Cambridge Elements

Elements in Evolutionary Economics
edited by
John Foster
University of Queensland
Jason Potts
RMIT University
Isabel Almudi
University of Zaragoza
Francisco Fatas-Villafranca
University of Zaragoza
David A. Harper
New York University

AGENT-BASED MACROECONOMICS

The Schumpeter Meeting Keynes Models

Giovanni Dosi
Sant'Anna School of Advanced Studies

Andrea Roventini
Sant'Anna School of Advanced Studies

Shaftesbury Road, Cambridge CB2 8EA, United Kingdom

One Liberty Plaza, 20th Floor, New York, NY 10006, USA

477 Williamstown Road, Port Melbourne, VIC 3207, Australia

314–321, 3rd Floor, Plot 3, Splendor Forum, Jasola District Centre,
New Delhi – 110025, India

103 Penang Road, #05–06/07, Visioncrest Commercial, Singapore 238467

Cambridge University Press is part of Cambridge University Press & Assessment, a department of the University of Cambridge.

We share the University's mission to contribute to society through the pursuit of education, learning and research at the highest international levels of excellence.

www.cambridge.org
Information on this title: www.cambridge.org/9781009598743
DOI: 10.1017/9781009414173

© Giovanni Dosi and Andrea Roventini 2025

This publication is in copyright. Subject to statutory exception and to the provisions of relevant collective licensing agreements, no reproduction of any part may take place without the written permission of Cambridge University Press & Assessment.

When citing this work, please include a reference to the DOI 10.1017/9781009414173

First published 2025

A catalogue record for this publication is available from the British Library

ISBN 978-1-009-59874-3 Hardback
ISBN 978-1-009-41421-0 Paperback
ISSN 2514-3573 (online)
ISSN 2514-3581 (print)

Additional resources for this publication at www.cambridge.org/EEVE_Roventini

Cambridge University Press & Assessment has no responsibility for the persistence or accuracy of URLs for external or third-party internet websites referred to in this publication and does not guarantee that any content on such websites is, or will remain, accurate or appropriate.

Agent-Based Macroeconomics

The Schumpeter Meeting Keynes Models

Elements in Evolutionary Economics

DOI: 10.1017/9781009414173
First published online: April 2025

Giovanni Dosi
Sant'Anna School of Advanced Studies

Andrea Roventini
Sant'Anna School of Advanced Studies

Author for correspondence: Andrea Roventini,
andrea.roventini@santannapisa.it

Abstract: This Element is about agent-based macroeconomics in general, and in particular about a family of evolutionary, agent-based models (ABMs), which are called 'Schumpeter meeting Keynes' (or K+S). The K+S models knit together 'Schumpeterian' endogenous processes of innovation with 'Keynesian' mechanisms of demand generation. As with all well-constructed ABMs, the K+S models are populated by a multiplicity of agents which interact on the grounds of quite simple, empirically based, behavioural rules, whose collective outcomes are 'emergent properties' which cannot be imputed to the intention of any single agent. After the K+S model is empirically validated, the impacts of different combinations of innovation, industrial, fiscal, and monetary policies for different labour-market regimes and inequality scenarios are assessed. The Element offers a new perspective on macroeconomics considering the economy as a complex evolving system.

Keywords: macroeconomics, agent-based computational economics, economic policy, business cycles, economic growth

© Giovanni Dosi and Andrea Roventini 2025

ISBNs: 9781009598743 (HB), 9781009414210 (PB), 9781009414173 (OC)
ISSNs: 2514-3573 (online), 2514-3581 (print)

Contents

1	Introduction	1
2	A Dismal Short Story of Macroeconomics: From Robinson Crusoe to Complex Evolutionary Economies	4
3	The Emperor Is Still Naked: The Intrinsic Limits of DSGE Models	14
4	Macroeconomic Agent-Based Models	24
5	The Schumpeter Meeting Keynes Model	32
6	Empirical Validation	47
7	Policy Experiments	59
8	A Brief Discussion on the Future of Macroeconomics by Way of a Conclusion	80
	Appendix A	86
	References	89

1 Introduction

This Element is about agent-based macroeconomics in general, and in particular about a family of evolutionary *Agent-Based Models (ABMs)*, which we call 'Schumpeter meeting Keynes' (or K+S). There are four fundamental features of the K+S family of agent-based models. The first is the complementarity between a Schumpeterian engine of innovation and a Keynesian engine of demand generation. Second, the models entail the intrinsic duality of wages, which are an item of cost for individual firms but also a component of aggregate demand. Third, there is a permanent duality between the labour-shedding effects of technical change via productivity improvements and its employment generation via the introduction of new products. Finally, fourth, ubiquitous institutions shape the rules of behaviours of individual agents and their pattern of interaction. As with all well-constructed ABMs, the K+S models are populated by a multiplicity of agents which interact on the grounds of quite simple, empirically based, behavioural rules, whose collective outcomes are 'emergent properties' which cannot be imputed to the intention of any single agent.

All this modelling perspective would sound quite straightforward were it not for the dismal state of current macroeconomics. Thus, given the latter, it might be appropriate to start by arguing why we need a 'macro' level of analysis well nested into valid microfoundations in the first place, which is perfectly obvious in all other natural and social disciplines, but not in economics. Next we shall place our presentation of ABMs against the background of the vicissitudes of modern macroeconomics as prolegomena to the core of this Element, the K+S family of macro ABMs.

With the noticeable exception of a good deal of contemporary economics, almost all scientific disciplines, both natural and social ones, distinguish between 'lower', more micro, levels of description of whatever phenomenon, and 'high-level' ones, regarding collective outcomes, which are typically *not isomorphic* to the former.[1] So, in physics, thermodynamics is not postulated on the kinetic properties of some 'representative' or 'average' molecules! And even more so in biology, ethology, or medicine. This is a fundamental point repeatedly emphasised by Kirman (2016) and outside our discipline by Anderson (1972) and Prigogine (1980), among a few outstanding others. The basic epistemological notion is that the *aggregate of interacting entities yields emergent properties*, which cannot be mapped down to the (conscious or

---

[1] More on these points in Dosi and Roventini (2019). See also Dosi (2012a), Fagiolo and Roventini (2017), and Dosi and Virgillito (2017) for further details.

unconscious) behaviours of some identifiable underlying components.[2] This is so obvious to natural scientists that it would be an insult to them to remind them that the dynamics of a beehive cannot be summarised by the dynamic adjustment of a 'representative bee' (the example is discussed, again, in Kirman, 2016). The relation between 'micro' and 'macro' has been at the very centre of all social sciences since their inception. Think of one of the everlasting questions, namely the relationship between *agency and structure*, which is at the core of most interpretations of social phenomena. Or, nearer to our concerns here, consider the (often misunderstood) notion of Adam Smith's *invisible hand*: this is basically a proposition about the lack of isomorphisms between the greediness of individual butchers and bakers, on the one hand, and the relatively orderly delivery of meat and bread across markets.

Unfortunately, what is obvious for the scientific community is unknown or ignored by current macroeconomics. Indeed, after a fruitful infancy in which the early Keynesian macroeconomic theories focused on the laws of motion of capitalist dynamics, also embedding some notions of disequilibrium and coordination failures, the discipline in the 1970s took a perverse path, relying on models grounded on fictitious rational representative agents in a pathetic attempt to circumvent aggregation and coordination problems. Such fraudulent microfoundations shrink the macro level to the optimising behaviour of one agent, thus losing all the complex dynamics emerging when one moves to the higher levels. The Dark Age of macroeconomics reached the abyss with the Great Recession of 2008, the biggest downturn that had hit developed economies since 1929. Not only was representative-agent macroeconomic theory unable to explain what happened in 2008, but it was instrumental to the crisis. Indeed, if macroeconomic models are grounded on a lonely agent, how could one study the rising of income inequality and financialisation which paved the way to the subprime mortgage crisis? A new macroeconomics paradigm is thus urgently needed.

In the new alternative paradigm, which inspires this Element, macroeconomics should consider the *economy as a complex, evolving system*, an ecology populated by heterogeneous agents (e.g. firms, workers, banks) whose far-from-equilibrium local interactions yield some collective order, even if the structure of the system continuously changes (more on that in Farmer & Foley, 2009; Kirman, 2010b, 2016; Rosser, 2011; Dosi, 2014, 2023; Dosi & Virgillito, 2017; Dosi & Roventini, 2019). In such a framework, first, *more is different* (Anderson, 1972): to repeat, there is not any isomorphism between the micro- and macroeconomic levels, and higher levels of aggregation can lead to the emergence of new phenomena (e.g. business cycles and self-sustained growth),

---

[2] A thorough discussion of emergence in economics is in Lane (1993).

new statistical regularities (e.g. Kaldor–Verdoorn and Okun's laws), and completely new structures (i.e. new firms, new industries, new markets, and new institutions).

Second, the economic system exhibits *self-organised criticality*: imbalances can build over time, leading to the emergence of tipping points which can be triggered by apparently innocuous shocks. (This is straightforward in climate change, see Steffen et al., 2018; but with regard to other fields in economics, see Bak et al., 1992 and Battiston et al., 2016.)

Third, in a complex world, *deep uncertainty* (Keynes, 1921, 1936; Knight, 1921; Dosi, 2023) is so pervasive that agents cannot build the 'right' model of the economy, and, even less so, share it among them as well as with the modeller (Kirman, 2014).

Fourth, behaviours typically rely on *heuristics* (Simon, 1955, 1959; Cyert & March,1992; Dosi, 2023), which turns out to be a robust set of tools for inference and actions (Gigerenzer & Brighton, 2009; Haldane, 2012; Dosi et al., 2020a).

Of course, fifth, local *interactions* among purposeful agents cannot be generally assumed to lead to efficient outcomes or optimal equilibria.

Finally, from a normative point of view, when complexity is involved, policy makers ought to aim at resilient systems which often require redundancy and degeneracy (Edelman & Gally, 2001). To put it in a provocative way: would someone fly on a plane designed by a team of New Classical macroeconomists, who sound much like the early aerodynamic scholars who conclusively argued that, in equilibrium, airplanes cannot fly?

Once complexity is seriously taken into account in macroeconomics, one, of course, has to rule out Dynamic Stochastic General Equilibrium (DSGE) models. A natural alternative candidate, we shall argue, is *Agent-Based Computational Economics* (ACE; Tesfatsion, 2006; LeBaron & Tesfatsion, 2008; Fagiolo & Roventini, 2017; Caverzasi & Russo, 2018; Dawid & Delli Gatti, 2018), which straightforwardly embeds heterogeneity, bounded rationality, endogenous out-of-equilibrium dynamics, and direct interactions among economic agents. In so doing, ACE provides an alternative way to build macroeconomic models with *genuine* microfoundations, which take seriously the problem of aggregation and are able to jointly account for the emergence of self-sustained growth and business cycles punctuated by major crises. Furthermore, on the normative side, due to the flexibility of their set of assumptions regarding agent behaviours and interactions, ACE models represent an exceptional laboratory to design policies and to test their effects on macroeconomic dynamics.

As recalled by Haldane and Turrell (2019), the first prototypes of agent-based models were developed by Enrico Fermi in the 1930s in order to study the movement of neutrons. (Of course, Fermi, a Nobel laureate physicist, never thought to build a model sporting a representative neutron!) With adoption of Monte Carlo methods, ABMs flourished in many disciplines, ranging from physics, biology, ecology, epidemiology, all the way to the military (more on that in Turrell, 2016). Recent years have also seen a surge of agent-based models in macroeconomics (see Fagiolo & Roventini, 2012, 2017 and Dawid & Delli Gatti, 2018 for surveys): an increasing number of papers involving macroeconomic ABMs have also addressed the policy domain concerning, for example, fiscal policy, monetary policy, macroprudential policy, labour market policy, and climate-change policy. And ABMs have been increasingly part of the policy tools in, for example, central banks and other institutions in ways complementary to older macroeconomic models (Haldane & Turrell, 2019).[3]

The rest of the Element is organised as follows. In Section 2, we will provide a short story of macroeconomics focusing on the problem of aggregation and, more generally, on its relationship with microeconomics. Section 3 discusses the insurmountable limits of neoclassical macroeconomics, focusing on its latest incarnation, the DSGE models. In Section 4 we introduce agent-based macroeconomics, and in Section 5 we present the family of Keynes meeting Schumpeter agent-based models. The empirical validation of the K+S models is performed in Section 6, while the impacts of different combinations of innovation, industrial, fiscal, and monetary policies for different labour-market regimes and inequality scenarios are assessed in Section 7. Finally, in Section 8 we conclude with a brief discussion on the future of macroeconomics.

2 A Dismal Short Story of Macroeconomics: From Robinson Crusoe to Complex Evolutionary Economies

The relationship between the micro and the macro is at the core of the (lack of) evolution of macroeconomics and it has a fundamental role in explaining why the 2008 financial crisis was also a crisis for macroeconomic theory (Kirman, 2010b). Indeed, standard DSGE models not only failed to forecast the crisis, but they did not even admit the possibility of such an event, leaving policy makers without policy solutions (Krugman, 2011). In this section, we briefly outline the path that macroeconomics has been following for the last ninety

---

[3] A growing and non-exhaustive list includes the Bank of England (Braun-Munzinger, Liu, & Turrell, 2016; Carro et al., 2022) the European Central Bank (Montagna & Kok, 2016; Halaj, 2018); Central Bank of Brazil (Da Silva & Tadeu Lima, 2015; Dos Santos & Nakane, 2017); Central Bank of Hungary (Hosszu & Mero, 2017); Bank of Russia (Ponomarenko & Sinyakov, 2018); the IMF (Chan-Lau, 2017); US Office of Financial Research (Bookstaber & Paddrik, 2015); the US Internal Revenue Service (Bloomquist & Koehler, 2015).

years (Sections 2.1–2.4).[4] Together, we will shed light on the dismal status of the discipline, which appears incapable of explaining the phenomena – that is, crises and depressions – for which it was born (see Section 2.5).

2.1 The Happy Childhood of Macroeconomics

Roughly speaking, macroeconomics first saw the light of day with Keynes. For sure, enlightening analyses came before, including Wicksell's, but the distinctiveness of macro levels of interpretation came with him. Indeed, up to the 1970s, there were basically two 'macros'.

One was equilibrium growth theories. While it is the case that, for example, models á la Solow invoked maximising behaviours in order to establish equilibrium input intensities, no claim was made that such allocations were the work of any 'representative agent' in turn taken to be the 'synthetic' (??) version of some underlying General Equilibrium (GE). By the same token, the distinction between positive (that is, purportedly descriptive) and normative models, before Lucas and his companions, was absolutely clear to the practitioners. Hence, the prescriptive side was kept distinctly separated. Ramsey (1928) – type models, asking what a benevolent central planner would do, were reasonably kept apart from any question on the 'laws of motion' of capitalism, á la Harrod (1939), Domar (1946), Kaldor (1957), and indeed Solow (1956). Finally, in the good and in the bad, technological change was kept separate from the mechanisms of resource allocation: the famous 'Solow residual' was, as is well known, the statistical counterpart of the drift in growth models with an exogenous technological change.

Second, in some fuzzy land between purported GE 'microfoundations' and equilibrium growth theories, lived for at least three decades a macroeconomics sufficiently 'Keynesian' in spirit and quite neoclassical in terms of tools. It was the early 'neo-Keynesianism' (also known as the Neoclassical Synthesis) – pioneered by Hicks (1937), and shortly thereafter by Modigliani, Samuelson, Patinkin, and a few other American 'Keynesians' – whom Joan Robinson contemptuously defined as 'bastard Keynesians'. It is the short-term macro which students used to learn up to the 1980s, with IS-LM curves, which are meant to capture the aggregate relations between money supply and money demand, interest rates, savings, and investments; Phillips curves on the labour market; and a few other curves as well. In fact, the curves were (are) a precarious compromise between the notion that the economy is supposed to be in some sort of equilibrium – albeit of a short-term nature – and the notion of a

---

[4] This section is partially grounded on Dosi & Roventini (2019).

more 'fundamental' equilibrium path to which the economy is bound to tend in the longer run.

That was a kind of mainstream, especially on the other side of the Atlantic. There was also a group of thinkers whom we could call (as they called themselves) *genuine Keynesians*. They were predominantly in Europe, especially in the UK and in Italy: see Pasinetti (1974, 1983) and Harcourt (2007) for an overview.[5] The focus was *only* on the basic *laws of motions* of *capitalist dynamics*. They include the drivers of aggregate demand; the multiplier leading from the 'autonomous' components of demand such as government expenditures and exports to aggregate income; the accelerator, linking aggregate investment to past variations in aggregate income itself; and the relation between unemployment, wage/profits shares, and investments.[6] Indeed, such a stream of research is alive and progressing, refining upon the modelling of the 'laws of motion' and their supporting empirical evidence: see Lavoie (2009); Lavoie and Stockhammer (2013); and Storm and Naastepad (2012a, 2012b), among quite a few others.

Indeed, a common characteristic of the variegated contributions from 'genuine Keynesianism', often known also as post-Keynesian, is the scepticism about any microfoundation, to its own merit and also to its own peril. Part of the denial comes from a healthy rejection of methodological individualism and its axiomatisation as the ultimate primitive of economic analysis. Part of it, in our view, comes from the misleading notion that microfoundations necessarily mean methodological individualism (as if the interpretation of the working of a beehive had to necessarily build upon the knowledge of 'what individual bees think and do', or indeed 'should do'). On the contrary, microfoundations might well mean how the macro structure of the beehive influences the distribution of the behaviours of the bees, a sort of *macrofoundation of the micro*. All this entails a major terrain of dialogue between the foregoing stream of Keynesian models and agent-based ones.

Now, back to the roots of modern macroeconomics. The opposite extreme to 'bastard Keynesianism' was not Keynesian at all, even if it sometimes took up the IS-LM-Phillips discourse. The best concise synthesis is Friedman (1968). Historically it went under the heading of *monetarism*, but basically it was the pre-Keynesian view that the economy left to itself travels on a unique equilibrium path *in the long- and short-run*. Indeed, in a barter, pre-industrial economy

---

[5] A sharp Economics-101 synthesis is Harcourt, Karmel, and Wallace (1967). A discussion of the 'Italian Keynesianism' and its links with the later Italian agent-based models is in Dosi and Roventini (2017).

[6] An early formalisation is via some Lotka–Volterra dynamics: see Goodwin (1950, 1951) and some refinements that one of the authors of this Element proposes in Dosi, Sodini, and Virgillito (2015).

where Say's law and the quantitative theory of money hold, monetary policy cannot influence the interest rate and fiscal policy completely crowds out private consumption and investment: 'there is a natural rate of unemployment which policies cannot influence'; see the deep discussion in Solow (2018). Milton Friedman was the obvious ancestor of Lucas and his companions, but he was still too far from the subsequent axioms, awaiting any empirical proof of plausibility.[7]

2.2 'New Classical (??)' Talibanism and Beyond

What happened next? Starting from the beginning of the 1970s, we think that everything which could get worse got worse and more: accordingly, we agree with Krugman (2011) and Romer (2016) that macroeconomics plunged into a Dark Age.[8]

First, 'new classical economics' (even if the reference to the Classics could not be further far away) fully abolished the distinction between the normative and positive domains – between models á la Ramsey and models á la Harrod-Domar, Solow, and so on (notwithstanding the differences amongst the latter ones). In fact, the striking paradox for theorists who are in good part market talibans is that they start with a model which is essentially of a benign, forward-looking, central planner, and only at the end, by way of an abundant dose of hand-waving, claim that the solution of whatever intertemporal optimisation problem is in fact supported by a decentralised market equilibrium.

Things could be much easier for this approach if one could build a genuine 'general equilibrium' model (that is, with many agents, heterogeneous at least in their endowments and preferences). However, this is not possible for the well-known, but ignored Sonnenschein (1972), Mantel (1974), and Debreu (1974) theorems (more in Kirman, 1989). Assuming by construction that the coordination problem is solved by resorting to the 'representative agent' fiction is simply a pathetic shortcut which does not have any theoretical legitimacy (Kirman, 1992).

---

[7] Nonetheless, Friedman was the pusher who first spread crack in the economic profession. Indeed, the core of monetarism has been absorbed into macroeconomics and it is the backbone of New Keynesian economics (Mankiw & Romer, 1991): e.g., the exogenous nature of business cycles, the natural rate of unemployment, the long-run neutrality of money, the limited efficacy of stabilisation policies, and the importance of rules rather than discretion. The monetarist Weltanschauung is so pervasive in modern macroeconomics that Bernanke (2002) celebrated Friedman's 90th birthday saying: 'Regarding the Great Depression. You're right, we did it. We're very sorry. But thanks to you, we won't do it again.' In that sense, monetarism has triumphed (De Long, 2000).

[8] For a much more detailed reconstruction of what happened to the theory, intertwined with the reconstruction of the actual policy dynamics which led to the 2008 crisis, see Cassidy (2009), Turner (2010), and Bookstaber (2017).

Anyhow, the 'New Classical' restoration went so far as to wash away the distinction between 'long-term' and 'short-term' – with the latter as the locus where all 'frictions', 'liquidity traps', Phillips curves, some (temporary!) real effects of fiscal and monetary policies, and so on had precariously survived before. Why would a representative agent endowed with 'rational' expectations able to solve sophisticated inter-temporal optimization problems from here to infinity display any friction or distortion in the short-run, if competitive markets always clear? We all know the outrageously silly propositions, sold as major discoveries, also associated with an infamous 'rational expectation revolution' concerning the ineffectiveness of fiscal and monetary policies and the general properties of markets to yield Pareto first-best allocations. (In this respect, of course, it is easier for that to happen if 'the market' is one representative agent: coordination and allocation failures would involve serious episodes of schizophrenia by that agent itself!).

While Lucas and Sargent 1978 wrote an obituary of Keynesian macroeconomics, we think that in other times, nearly the entire profession would have reacted to such a 'revolution' as Bob Solow once did when asked by Klamer (1984) why he did not take the 'new Classics' seriously:

> Suppose someone sits down where you are sitting right now and announces to me he is Napoleon Bonaparte. The last thing I want to do with him is to get involved in a technical discussion of cavalry tactics at the battle of Austerlitz. If I do that, I am tacitly drawn in the game that he is Napoleon. Now, Bob Lucas and Tom Sargent like nothing better than to get drawn in technical discussions, because then you have tacitly gone along with their fundamental assumptions; your attention is attracted away from the basic weakness of the whole story. Since I find that fundamental framework ludicrous, I respond by treating it as ludicrous — that is, by laughing at it — so as not to fall in the trap of taking it seriously and passing on matters of technique. (Solow in Klamer, 1984, p. 146)

The reasons why the profession, and even worse, the world at large took these 'Napoleons' seriously, we think, have basically to do with a Zeitgeist where the hegemonic politics was that epitomized by Ronald Reagan and Margaret Thatcher, and their system of beliefs on the 'magic of the market place', 'society does not exist, only individuals do', et similia. And, tragically, this set of beliefs became largely politically bipartisan, leading to financial deregulation, massive waves of privatisation, tax cuts and surging inequality, and so on. Or think of the disasters produced for decades around the world by the IMF-inspired Washington Consensus or by the latest waves of austerity and structural-reform policies in the European Union as another such creed on the magic of markets, the evil of governments, and the miraculous effects of blood, sweat, and tears (Fitoussi & Saraceno, 2013, refers to this as the

Berlin–Washington consensus). The point we want to make is that the changes in the hegemonic (macro) theory should be primarily interpreted in terms of the political economy of power relations among social and political groups, with little to write home about 'advancements' in the theory itself... On the contrary!

The Mariana Trench of fanaticism was reached with Real Business Cycle (RBC) models (Kydland & Prescott, 1982) positing optimal Pareto business cycles driven by economywide technological shocks [*sic*]. The natural question immediately arising concerns the nature of such shocks. What are they? Are recessions driven by episodes of technological regress (e.g. people going back to wash clothes in rivers or suddenly using candles for lighting)? The candid answer provided by one of the founding fathers of RBC theory is that: 'They're that traffic out there' ('there' refers to a congested bridge, meaning some mysterious crippling of the 'invisible hand', as cited in Romer, 2016, p. 5). Needless to say, the RBC propositions were (and are) not supported by any empirical evidence. But the price paid by macroeconomics for this sort of intellectual trolling was and still is huge!

2.3 New Keynesians, New Monetarists and the New Neoclassical Synthesis

Since the 1980s, 'New Keynesian' economists, instead of following Solow's advices,[9] basically accepted the New Classical and RBC framework and worked on the edges of auxiliary assumptions. So, they introduced monopolistic competition and a plethora of nominal and real rigidities into models with representative-agent cum rational-expectations microfoundations. New Keynesian models restored some basic results which were undisputed before the New Classical Middle Ages, such as the non-neutrality of money. However, the price paid to talk just to 'New Classicals' and RBC talibans was tall. The methodological infection was so deep that Mankiw and Romer (1991) claimed that New Keynesian macroeconomics should be renamed New Monetarist macroeconomics, and De Long (2000) discussed 'the triumph of monetarism'. 'New Keynesianism' of different vintages represents what we could call *homeopathic Keynesianism*: the minimum quantities to be added to the standard model, sufficient to mitigate the most outrageous claims of the latter.

Indeed, the widespread sepsis came with the appearance of a New Neoclassical Synthesis (NNS) (Goodfriend, 2007), grounded upon DSGE models (Clarida, Galí, & Gertler, 1999; Woodford, 2003; Galí & Gertler, 2007). In a nutshell, such models have a RBC core supplemented with monopolistic competition, nominal imperfections, and a monetary policy rule, and they can

---
[9] And the warnings of Kaldor (1982) against the 'Scourge of Monetarism'.

accomodate various forms of 'imperfections', 'frictions', and 'inertias'. To many respects DSGE models are simply the late-Ptolemaic phase of the theory: add epicycles at full steam without any theoretical and empirical discipline in order to better match a particular set of the data. Of course, in the epicycles frenzy one is never touched by a sense of the ridiculous in assuming that the mythical representative agent at the same time is extremely sophisticated when thinking about future allocations, but falls into backward-looking habits when deciding about consumption or, when having to change prices, is tangled by sticky prices! (Caballero, 2010, offers a thorough picture of this surreal state of affairs.) Again, Bob Solow gets straight to the point:[10]

> But I found the advent of – Dynamic Stochastic General Equilibrium models to be, not so much as a step backwards, but as a step out of economics. In fact, I've been criticized, probably justly, for making jokes about it, but it struck me as funny, as not something you could take seriously. There were times when you start reading an article in that vein, and it would start by saying, "Well, we are going to write down a micro-founded model." It meant an economy with one person in it, and organized so that the economy carried out the wishes of that person. Well, when I was growing up and getting interested in economics, the essence of economics was that there were people and groups of people in the economy who had conflicting interests. Not only did they want different things, opposing things, they believed different things. And there's no place for that in what passes, or what was passing a dozen years ago, for a micro-founded model.

Not all New Keynesian economists deliberately choose to step out of economics. Indeed, 'New Keynesianism' is a misnomer, in that sometimes it is meant to cover also simple but quite powerful models whereby Keynesian system properties are obtained out of otherwise standard microfoundations, just taking seriously 'imperfections' as structural, long-term characteristics of the economy. Pervasive asymmetric information requires some genuine heterogeneity and interactions among agents (see Akerlof & Yellen, 1985; Greenwald & Stiglitz, 1993a, 1993b; Akerlof, 2002, 2007, among others) yielding Keynesian properties as ubiquitous outcomes of coordination failures (for more detailed discussions of Stiglitz's contributions, see Dosi & Virgillito, 2017).[11] All that, still without considering the long-term changes in the so-called fundamentals, technical progress, and so on.

---

[10] The whole interview can be found here:
https://freakonomics.com/podcast/ninety-eight-years-of-economic-wisdom/.

[11] See also the seminal contribution of Leijonhufvud (1968) for an interpretation of Keynesian theory grounded on market disequilibrium processes and coordination failures.

2.4 What about Innovation Dynamics and Long-Run Economic Growth?

We have argued that even the coordination issue has been written out of the agenda by assuming it as basically solved by construction. But what about change? What about the 'Unbound Prometheus' (Landes, 1969) of capitalist search, discovery, and indeed destruction?

In Solow (1956) and subsequent contributions, technical progress appears by default, but it does so in a powerful way as the fundamental driver of long-run growth, to be explained outside the sheer allocation mechanism.[12] On the contrary, in the DSGE workhorse, there is no Prometheus: 'innovations' come as exogenous technology shocks upon the aggregate production function, with the same mythical agent optimally adjusting its consumption and investment plans. And the macroeconomic time series generated by the models are usually de-trended to focus on their business cycle dynamics.[13] End of the story.

The last thirty years have seen also the emergence of *new growth theories* (see e.g. Romer, 1990; Aghion & Howitt, 1992), bringing – as compared to the original Solow model – some significant advancements and, in our view, equally significant drawbacks. The big plus is the endogenisation of technological change: innovation is endogenised into economic dynamics. But that is done just as either a learning externality or as the outcome of purposeful expensive efforts by profit-maximising agents. In the latter case, the endogenisation comes at what we consider the major price (although many colleagues would deem it as a major achievement) of reducing innovative activities to an equilibrium outcome of optimal intertemporal allocation of resources, with or without (probabilisable) uncertainty. Hence, by doing that, one loses also the genuine Schumpeterian notion of innovation as a disequilibrium phenomenon (at least as a transient!).

Moreover, 'endogenous growth' theories do not account for business cycles' fluctuations. This is really unfortunate, as Bob Solow (2005) puts it:

> Neoclassical growth theory is about the evolution of potential output. In other words, the model takes it for granted that aggregate output is limited on the supply side, not by shortages (or excesses) of effective demand. Short-run macroeconomics, on the other hand, is mostly about the gap between potential and actual output. ... Some sort of endogenous knitting-together of the

---

[12] In this respect there has always been a great sense of complementarity by Solow with Schumpeter and, later on, Nelson and Winter (1982). And conversely a somewhat reductionist interpretation of Nelson and Winter's contribution could be a long-term microfoundation of Solow's dynamics.

[13] Exogenous total-factor productivity (TFP) shocks in the production function are modeled in order to deliver a unit root in the productivity and output time series.

> fluctuations and growth contexts is needed, and not only for the sake of neatness: the short run and its uncertainties affect the long run through the volume of investment and research expenditure, for instance, and the growth forces in the economy probably influence the frequency and amplitude of short-run fluctuations. ... To put it differently, it would be a good thing if there were a unified macroeconomics capable of dealing with trend and fluctuations, rather than a short-run branch and a long-run branch operating under quite different rules. My quarrel with the real business cycle and related schools is not about that; it is about whether they have chosen an utterly implausible unifying device. (Solow, 2005, pp. 5–6)

And the separation between growth and business cycle theories is even more problematic given the bourgeoning new empirical literature on *hysteresis* (among many others, see Dosi et al., 2018a; Cerra, Fatás, & Saxena 2023, and the literature cited therein), which convincingly shows the existence of many interlinkages between short-run and long-run phenomena. In particular, in the presence of hysteresis, recessions can permanently depress output, thus undermining the very growing capabilities of economies. On the policy side, this calls for a more active role of fiscal and monetary interventions during downturns, and, more generally, to consider the impact of policies across the whole spectrum of frequencies. On the theoretical side, hysteresis is not due to market imperfections, but rather to the very functioning of decentralised economies characterised by coordination externalities and dynamic increasing returns. In that respect, this Element shows that evolutionary agent-based models are genuinely able to account for the emergence of hysteresis, while providing a unified analysis of technological change and long-run growth together with coordination failures and business cycles.

2.5 From the 'Great Moderation' to the Great Recession

In the beginning of this century, under the new consensus reached by the New Neoclassical Synthesis (NNS), Robert E. Lucas, Jr, (2003) without any embarrassment, declared 'The central problem of depression prevention had been solved', and Prescott religiously believed that: 'This is the golden age of macroeconomics'.[14] Moreover, a large number of NNS contributions claimed that economic policy was finally becoming more of a science (!?), (Galí & Gertler, 2007; Goodfriend, 2007; Mishkin, 2007; Taylor, 2007).[15] This was made possible by the ubiquitous presence of DSGE models in academia and a

---

[14] See Prescott's lecture at Trinity University in San Antonio, Texas (April 2006): www.trinity edu/ nobel/Prescott/Prescott_Webquotes.htm.

[15] An exception was Howitt (2012) who claimed that 'macroeconomic theory has fallen behind the practice of central banking' (p. 2).

universe of politicians and opinion-makers under the 'free market' / 'free Wall Street' globalization spell,[16] and helped by the 'divine coincidence', whereby inflation targeting, performed under some form of Taylor rule, appeared to be a sufficient condition for stabilising the whole economy. During this Panglossian period, some economists went as far as claiming that the 'scientific approach' to macroeconomics policy incarnated in DSGE models was the ultimate cause of the so-called Great Moderation (Bernanke, 2004), namely the fall of GDP volatility experienced by most developed economists since the beginning of the 1980s, and that only minor refinements to the consensus workhorse model were needed.

Unfortunately, as happened with the famous statement made by Francis Fukuyama (1992) about an alleged 'end of history',[17] these positions have been proven to be substantially wrong by subsequent events. Indeed, a relatively small 'micro' event, the bankruptcy of Lehman Brothers in 2008, triggered a major financial crisis which caused the Great Recession, the deepest downturn experienced by developed economies since 1929.

In that respect, the Great Recession turned out to be a 'natural experiment' for economic analysis, showing the inadequacy of the predominant theoretical frameworks. Indeed, as Krugman (2011) points out, not only did DSGE models not forecast the crisis, but they did not even admit the possibility of such an event and, even worse, they did not provide any useful advice to policymakers on how to put the economy back on a steady growth path (see also Turner, 2010; Stiglitz, 2011, 2015; Bookstaber, 2017; Caverzasi & Russo, 2018; Haldane & Turrell, 2019).

Scholars of DSGE have reacted to such a failure by trying to amend their models with a new legion of epicycles; for example, financial frictions, homeopathic doses of agent heterogeneity, bounded rationality, and exogenous fat-tailed shocks (see e.g. Lindé, Smets, & Wouters, 2016, and the discussion

---

[16] Chari, Kehoe, and McGrattan (2009) put it in the clearest way: 'an aphorism among macroeconomists today is that if you have a coherent story to propose, you can do it in a suitably elaborate DSGE model'.

[17] Recently Fukuyama updated his opinion: 'If you mean [by socialism] redistributive programs that try to redress this big imbalance in both incomes and wealth that has emerged then, yes, I think not only can it come back, it ought to come back. This extended period, which started with Reagan and Thatcher, in which a certain set of ideas about the benefits of unregulated markets took hold, in many ways it's had a disastrous effect. In social equality, it's led to a weakening of labour unions, of the bargaining power of ordinary workers, the rise of an oligarchic class almost everywhere that then exerts undue political power. In terms of the role of finance, if there's anything we learned from the financial crisis it's that you've got to regulate the sector like hell because they'll make everyone else pay. That whole ideology became very deeply embedded within the Eurozone, the austerity that Germany imposed on southern Europe has been disastrous.' Interview on the New Statesman, 17 Oct 2018, www.newstatesman.com/culture/observations/2018/10/francis-fukuyama-interview-socialism-ought-come-back.

in Section 3.4). Conversely, an increasing number of economists have claimed that the 2008 'economic crisis is a crisis for economic theory' (Colander et al., 2009; Farmer & Foley, 2009; Krugman, 2009, 2011; Caballero, 2010; Kirman, 2010b, 2016; Kay, 2011; Stiglitz, 2011, 2015; Dosi, 2014; Romer, 2016; Stiglitz, 2017). Indeed, history is the smoking gun against the deeply flawed basic assumptions of mainstream DSGE macroeconomics, for example rational expectations and representative agents, which prevents, by construction, the understanding of the emergence of deep downturns together with standard fluctuations (Stiglitz, 2015) and, more generally, the very dynamics of economies. Indeed, resorting to representative-agent microfoundations, how can one understand central phenomena such as rising inequality, bankruptcy cascades and systemic risks, innovation, structural change, and their co-evolution with climate dynamics?

3 The Emperor Is Still Naked: The Intrinsic Limits of DSGE Models

In line with the RBC tradition, the backbone of DSGE models (Clarida et al., 1999; Woodford, 2003; Galí & Gertler, 2007) is a standard stochastic equilibrium model with variable labour supply: the economy is populated by an infinitely everlasting representative household, and by a representative firm, whose homogenous production technology is hit by exogenous shocks.[18] All agents form their expectations rationally (Muth, 1961). The New Keynesian flavor of the model is provided by money, monopolistic competition, and sticky prices. Money has usually only the function of unit of account, and the nominal rigidities incarnated in sticky prices allow monetary policy to affect real variables in the short run. The RBC scaffold of the model allows the computation of the 'natural' level of output and real interest rate, that is, the equilibrium values of the two variables under perfectly flexible prices. In line with the Wicksellian tradition, the 'natural' output and interest rate constitute a benchmark for monetary policy: the central bank cannot persistently push the output and the interest rate away from their 'natural' values without creating inflation or deflation. Finally, imperfect competition and possibly other real rigidity imply that the 'natural' level of output might not be socially efficient.

Dynamic Stochastic General Equilibrium models are commonly represented by means of vector auto-regression (VAR) models usually estimated by employing full-information Bayesian techniques (see e.g. Smets & Wouters, 2003, 2007). Different types of shocks are usually added to improve the estimation. Moreover, as the assumption of forward-looking agents prevents

---

[18] This section is grounded on Fagiolo and Roventini 2017 and Dosi and Roventini 2019.

DSGE models from matching the econometric evidence on the co-movements of nominal and real variables (e.g., the response of output and inflation to a monetary policy shock is too fast to match the gradual adjustment showed by the corresponding empirical impulse-response functions), a legion of 'frictions' – generally not justified on theoretical grounds – is introduced, such as predetermined price and spending decisions, indexation of prices and wages to past inflation, sticky wages, habit formation in preferences for consumption, adjustment costs in investment, variable capital utilization, among others. Once the parameters of the model are estimated and the structural shocks are identified, policy-analysis exercises are carried out assuming that the DSGE model is the 'true' data-generating process of the available time series.

The usefulness of DSGE models is undermined by plenty of theoretical, empirical, and political-economy problems. Let us discuss each of them in turn (see Fagiolo & Roventini, 2017, for a more detailed analysis).

3.1 Theoretical Issues

As already mentioned previously, DSGE models suffer the same well-known problems as Arrow–Debreu general-equilibrium models (see Kirman, 1989, for a classical reference) *and more*. Neglecting them does not mean solving them. On the contrary!

More specifically, the well-known Sonnenschein (1972), Mantel (1974), and Debreu (1974) theorems show that neither the uniqueness nor, and even less so, the stability of the general equilibrium can be attained, even if one employs stringent and unrealistic assumptions about agents, even under amazing information requirements. Indeed, Saari and Simon (1978) show that an infinite amount of information is required to reach the equilibrium for any initial price vector.

The representative agent (RA) shortcut has been taken to circumvent any aggregation problem. The RA assumption implies that there is isomorphism between micro- and macro-economics, with the latter shrunk to the former. This, of course, is far from being innocent: there are (at least) four reasons for which it cannot be defended (Kirman, 1992).[19]

First, individual rationality does not imply 'aggregate rationality': one cannot provide any formal justification to support the assumption that the macro level behaves as a maximising individual.

---

[19] A discussion of the limits of the representative assumption in light of the current crisis is contained in Kirman (2010b).

Second, even if one forgets also that one cannot safely perform policy analyses with RA macro models, the reactions of the representative agent to shocks or parameter changes may not coincide with the aggregate reactions of the represented agents.

Third, the lack of micro/macro isomorphism is revealed even in terms of aggregation of preferences: the representative agent might appear to prefer a, even if all the 'represented' individuals might well prefer b.

Fourth, the RA assumption also induces additional difficulties on testing grounds, because whenever one tests a proposition delivered by a RA model, one is also jointly testing the very RA hypothesis. Hence, one tests the rejection of the latter together with the rejection of the specific model proposition (more on that in Forni & Lippi, 1997, 1999; Pesaran & Chudik, 2014).

Finally, the last theoretical issue concerns the existence and determinacy of the system of rational-expectation equilibrium conditions of DSGE models. If the exogenous shocks and the fluctuations generated by the monetary policy rule are 'small', and the 'Taylor principle' holds, the rational-expectation equilibrium of the DSGE model exists and is locally determinate (Woodford, 2003). This result allows one to compute impulse-response functions in the presence of 'small' shocks or parameter changes and to safely employ log-linear approximations around the steady state. Unfortunately, the existence of a local determinate equilibrium does not rule out the possibility of multiple equilibria at the global level (see e.g. Schmitt-Grohè & Uribe, 2000; Benhabib, Schmitt-Grohè, & Uribe, 2001; Ascari & Ropele, 2009). This is a serious issue because there is always the possibility, for example if the laws of motion of the shocks are not properly tuned, that the DSGE model enters in an explosive path, thus preventing the computation of impulse-response functions and the adoption of the model for policy analysis exercises.

3.2 Empirical Issues

Even neglecting the theoretical absurdities of the basic DSGE edifice, already mentioned previously, equally serious pitfalls concern their empirical use.

The estimation and testing of DSGE models are usually performed assuming that they represent the 'true' data generating process (DGP) of the observed data (Canova, 2008). This implies that the ensuing inference and policy experiments are valid only if the DSGE model mimics the unknown DGP of the data.[20] Notice that such an epistemology widespread in economics but unique to it (and to theology!), *assumes* that the world is 'transparent' and thus the 'model' faithfully reflects it. This is well epitomised by the grotesque

---

[20] On this and related points addressing the statistical vs. substantive adequacy of DSGE models, see Poudyal and Spanos (2013).

Scientology-like remark of Sargent about rational expectations: 'All agents inside the model, the econometrician, and God share the same model' (Sargent, 2005). All other scientific disciplines are basically there to conjecture, verify, and falsify models of the world. Not our own! So, also concerning DSGE models, their econometric performance is assessed along the identification, estimation, and evaluation dimensions (Fukac & Pagan, 2006).

Given the large number of non-linearities present in the structural parameters, DSGE models are hard to identify (Canova, 2008). This leads to a large number of identification problems, which can affect the parameter space either at the local or at the global level.[21] Identification problems lead to biased and fragile estimates of some structural parameters and do not allow one to rightly evaluate the significance of the estimated parameters applying standard asymptotic theories. This opens a ridge between the real and the DSGE DGP, depriving parameter estimates of any economic meaning and making policy analysis exercises useless (Canova, 2008).

Such identification problems also affect the estimation of DGSE models. Bayesian methods apparently address the estimation (and identification) issues by adding a prior function to the (log) likelihood function in order to increase the curvature of the latter and obtain a smoother function. However, this choice is not harmless: if the likelihood function is flat – and thus conveys little information about the structural parameters – the shape of the posterior distribution resembles the one of the prior, reducing estimation to a more sophisticated calibration procedure carried out on an interval instead of on a point (see Fukac & Pagan, 2006; Canova, 2008). Indeed, the likelihood functions produced by most DSGE models are quite flat (see e.g. the exercises performed by Fukac & Pagan, 2006).[22]

Evaluating a DSGE model, as well as any other models, implies in principle assessing its capability to reproduce a large set of stylized facts, in our case macroeconomic ones (microeconomic regularities cannot be attained by construction given the representative-agent assumption). Fukac and Pagan (2006) performed such exercises on a popular DSGE model with disappointing results. Moreover, DSGE models might seem to do well in 'normal' time, but they cannot account even in principle for crises and deep downturns (Stiglitz, 2015), even when fat-tailed shocks are assumed (Ascari, Fagiolo, & Roventini, 2015).[23]

---

[21] A taxonomy of the most relevant identification problems can be found in Canova and Sala (2009). See also Beyer and Farmer (2004) and the discussion in Romer (2016).

[22] In this case, informal calibration is a more modest but honest strategy for policy analysis (Canova, 2008).

[23] As Alan Kirman puts it, this is like a theory stating that 'in the twentieth century Germany has been a country peaceful most of the time'.

The results just described seem to support Favero's (2007) claim that modern DSGE models are exposed to the same criticisms advanced against the old-fashioned macroeconometric models belonging to the Cowles Commission tradition: they pay too much attention to the identification of the structural model (with all the problems described earlier) without testing the potential misspecification of the underlying statistical model (see also Johansen, 2006; Juselius & Franchi, 2007). If the statistical model is misspecified, policy analysis exercises lose significance, because they are carried out in a 'virtual' world whose data-generating process is different from the one underlying observed time-series data.

More generally, the typical assertion made by DSGE modelers that their theoretical frameworks are able to replicate real-world evidence is at odds with a careful scrutiny of how the empirical evaluation of DSGE models is actually done. Dynamic Stochastic General Equilibrium modelers, indeed, typically select ex ante the set of empirical criteria that their models should satisfy in such a way as to be sure that these restrictions are met. However, they usually refrain from confronting their models with the wealth of fundamental features of growth over the capitalist business cycles, which DSGE models are not structurally able to replicate.

3.3 Political-Economy Issues

Given the theoretical problems and the puny empirical performance of DSGE models, their assumptions cannot be defended by invoking arguments either of parsimonious modelling or data matching. This opens a Pandora's box on the links between the legion of assumptions of DSGE models and their policy conclusions. But behind all that, one of the crucial issues concerns the relationship between the information the representative agent is able to access, 'the model of the world' she has, and her ensuing behaviours.

Dynamic Stochastic General Equilibrium models assume a very peculiar framework, whereby representative agents are endowed with a sort of 'olympic' rationality, and have free access to an unbounded information set.[24] Moreover, rational expectation is the common shortcut employed by DSGE models to deal with uncertainty. Such utterly strong assumptions, however, raise more question marks than answers.

First, even assuming individual rationality, how does it carry over through aggregation, yielding rational expectations (RE) at the system level? For

---

[24] This is what mainstream macroeconomics consider 'sound microfoundations'. However, as Kirman (2016) put it: 'the rationality attributed to individuals is based on the introspection of economists rather than on careful empirical observation of how individuals actually behave'.

sure, individual rationality is not a sufficient condition for letting the system converge to the RE fixed-point equilibrium (Howitt, 2012). Relatedly, while it is in general unreasonable to assume that agents possess all the information required to attain the equilibrium of the whole economy (Caballero, 2010), this applies even more so to periods of strong structural transformation, like the Great Recession, that require policies never tried before (e.g. quantitative easing; see Stiglitz, 2011, 2015).

Second, agents can also have the 'wrong' model of the economy, but available data may corroborate it (see the seminal contribution of Woodford, 1990, among the rich literature on sunspots).

Third, as Hendry and Minzon (2010) point out, when 'structural breaks' affect the underlying stochastic process that governs the evolution of the economy, the learning process of agents introduces further non-stationarity into the system, preventing the economy from reaching an equilibrium state, if there is one. More generally, in the presence of genuine uncertainty (Keynes, 1936; Knight, 1921), 'rational' agents should follow heuristics, as they always outperform more complex expectation formation rules (Gigerenzer & Brighton, 2009; Dosi et al., 2020a). But, if this is so, then the modelers should assume that agents behave according to how the psychological and sociological evidence suggests that they actually behave (Akerlof, 2002; Akerlof & Shiller, 2009). Conversely, given such circumstances, it is no wonder that empirical tests usually reject the full-information, rational expectation hypothesis (see e.g. Coibion & Gorodnichenko, 2015; Gennaioli, Ma, & Shleifer, 2015).

The representative-agent (RA) assumption prevents DSGE models from reaching any distributional issue, even if they are intertwined with the major causes of the Great Recession and, more generally, they are fundamental for studying the effects of policies. So, for example, increasing inequalities in income (Atkinson, Piketty, & Saez, 2011) and wealth inequalities (Piketty & Zucman, 2014) might have contributed to inducing households to hold more and more debt, paving the way to the subprime mortgage crisis (Fitoussi & Saraceno, 2010; Stiglitz, 2011). Redistribution matters and different policies have a different impact on the economy according to the groups of people they are designed for (e.g. unemployed benefits have larger multipliers than do tax cuts for high-income individuals; see Stiglitz, 2011). However, the study of redistributive policies requires models with *heterogeneous* agents.

The RA assumption coupled with the implicit presence of a Walrasian auctioneer, which sets prices before exchanges take place, rules out by construction the possibility of interactions among heterogeneous individuals. This prevents DSGE models also from accurately studying the dynamics of credit and financial markets. Indeed, the assumption that the representative agent always satisfies the transversality condition removes the default risk from the models (Goodhart, 2009). As a consequence, agents face the same interest rate (no risk premia) and all transactions can be undertaken in capital markets without the need of banks. Abstracting from default risks prevents DSGE models from contemplating the conflict between price and financial stability faced by central banks (Howitt, 2012). As they do not consider the huge costs of financial crises, they deceptively appear to work fine only in 'normal' times (Stiglitz, 2011, 2015); basically when one does not need them!

In the same vein, DSGE models are not able to account for involuntary unemployment. Indeed, even if they are meant to study the welfare effects of macroeconomic policies, unemployment is not present or, when it is, it only stems from frictions in the labour market or from wage rigidities. Such explanations are especially hard to believe during deep downturns like, for example, the Great Recession. In DSGE models, the lack of heterogeneous, interacting firms and workers/consumers prevents the study of the possibility of massive coordination failures (Cooper & John, 1988; Leijonhufvud, 1968, 2000), which could lead to an insufficient level of aggregate demand and to involuntary unemployment.

In fact, the macroeconomics of DSGE models does not appear to be genuinely grounded on any microeconomics (Stiglitz, 2011, 2015) they do not even take into account the micro and macro implications of imperfect information, while the behaviour of agents is often described with arbitrary specifications of the functional forms (e.g. Dixit–Stiglitz utility function, Cobb–Douglas production function).

More generally, DSGE models suffer from a sort of internal contradiction. On the one hand, strong assumptions such as rational expectations, perfect information, and complete financial markets are introduced ex ante to provide a rigorous and formal mathematical treatment and to allow for policy recommendations. On the other hand, many imperfections (e.g., sticky prices, rule-of-thumb consumers) are introduced ex post without any theoretical justification only to allow the DSGE model to match the data (see also the discussion later in this Element). Along these lines Chari et al. (2009) argue that the high level of arbitrariness of DSGE models in the specifications of structural shocks may leave them exposed to the so-called Lucas critique, preventing them from being usefully employed for policy analysis.

An assumption of DSGE models is that business cycles stem from a plethora of exogenous shocks. As a consequence, DSGE models do not explain business cycles, preferring instead to postulate them as a sort of deus ex machina mechanism. This could explain why even in 'normal times' DSGE models are not able to match many business cycle stylized facts or need to assume serially correlated shocks to produce fluctuations resembling the ones observed in reality (cf. Zarnowitz, 1985, 1997; Cogley & Nason, 1993; Fukac & Pagan, 2006). Even worse, phenomena like the subprime mortgage crisis clearly show how bubbles and, more generally, *endogenously generated shocks* are far more important for understanding economic fluctuations (Stiglitz, 2011, 2015).

Moving to the normative side, one supposed advantage of the DSGE approach is the possibility of deriving optimal policy rules. However, when the 'true' model of the economy is not known, rule-of-thumb policy rules can perform better than optimal policy rules (Brock et al., 2007; Orphanides & Williams, 2008). Indeed, in complex worlds with pervasive uncertainty (e.g. in financial markets), policy rules should be simple (Haldane, 2012), while 'redundancy' and 'degeneracy' (Edelman & Gally, 2001) are required to achieve resiliency.

3.4 Post-Crisis DSGE Models: Some Fig Leaves Are Not a Cloth

The failure of DSGE models to account for the Great Recession sparked the search for refinements, which were also partly trying to address the critiques discussed in the previous three sections. More specifically, researchers in the DSGE camp have tried to include a financial sector into the barebones model, consider some forms of (very mild) heterogeneity and bounded rationality, and explore the impact of rare exogenous shocks on the performance of DSGE models.

Let us provide a bird's-eye view of such recent developments. (Another overview is Caverzasi & Russo, 2018.)

The new generation of DSGE model with *financial frictions* are mostly grounded on the so-called financial accelerator framework (Bernanke, Gertler, & Gilchrist, 1999), which provides a straightforward explanation why credit and financial markets can affect real economic activity. The presence of imperfect information between borrowers and lenders introduces a wedge between the cost of credit and those of internal finance. In turn, the balance-sheets of lenders and borrowers can affect the real sector via the supply of credit and the spread on loan interest rates (see Gertler & Kiyotaki, 2010, for a survey). For instance, Curdia and Woodford (2010) introduce patient and impatient consumers to justify the existence of a stylized financial intermediary, which copes with default risk charging a spread on its loan subject to exogenous, stochastic disturbances. From the policy side, they conclude that central banks should keep on controlling the short-term interest rate (see also Curdia & Woodford, 2016). In the model of Gertler and Karadi (2011), households can randomly become workers or bankers. In the latter case, they provide credit to firms, but as they are constrained by deposits and the resources they can raise in the interbank market, a spread emerges between loans' and deposits' interest rates (see also Christiano, Motto, & Rostagno, 2013). They find that during (exogenous) recessions, unconventional monetary policy (i.e. the central bank providing credit intermediation) is welfare enhancing (see also Gertler and Kiyotaki, 2010 and Curdia and Woodford, 2011 for other types of credit policies).

The foregoing contributions allow for some form of *mild heterogeneity* among agents. Some DSGE models consider two classes of agents in order to explore issues such as debt deflations or inequality. For instance, Eggertsson and Krugman (2012) introduce patient and impatient agents and expose the latter to exogenous debt limit shocks, which force them to deleverage. In such a framework, there can be debt deflations, liquidity traps, and fiscal policies can be effective. Kumhof, Ranciere, and Winant (2015) try to study the link between rising inequality and financial crises employing a DSGE model where exogenously imposed income distribution guarantees that top earner households (5% of the income distribution) lend to the bottom ones (95% of the income distribution). Exogenous shocks induce low-income households to increase their indebtedness, raising their 'rational' willingness to default and, in turn, the probability of a financial crisis. More recent works consider a continuum of heterogenous households in an incomplete market framework. For instance, in the Heterogenous Agent New Keynesian (HANK) model developed by Kaplan, Moll, and Violante (2018), the assumptions of uninsurable income shocks and multiple assets with different degrees of liquidity and returns lead to wealth distributions and marginal propensities to consume more in tune with the empirical evidence. In this framework, monetary policy is effective only if it provokes a general-equilibrium response of labour demand and household income, and as the Ricardian equivalence breaks down, its impact is intertwined with fiscal policy.

An increasing number of DSGE models allow for various forms of *bounded rationality* (see Dilaver, Jump, & Levine, 2018 for a survey) albeit to homeopathic degrees. In one stream of literature, agents know the equilibrium of the economy and form their expectations as if they were econometricians, by using the available observations to compute their parameter estimates via ordinary least square (in line with Evans & Honkapohja, 2001). Other recent contributions have relaxed the rational expectations assumption preserving maximisation (Woodford, 2013). For instance, an increasing number of works assume 'rational inattention', that is, optimising agents rationally decide not to use all the available information because they have finite processing capacity (Sims, 2010). Along this line, Gabaix (2014) models 'bounded rationality', assuming that agents have a simplified model of the world, but, nonetheless, they can jointly maximise their utility and their inattention. Drawing inspiration from artificial intelligence programs, Woodford (2018) develops a DSGE model where rational agents can forecast up to k steps ahead. Finally, building on Brock and Hommes (1997), in an increasing number of DSGE models, agents can form their expectations using an ecology of different learning rules, usually fundamentalist versus extrapolative rules (see e.g. Branch & McGough, 2011; De Grauwe, 2012; Anufriev et al., 2013; Massaro, 2013). As the fraction of agents following different expectations rules changes over time, 'small' shocks can give rise to persistent and asymmetric fluctuations and endogenous business cycles may arise.

Finally, a new generation of DSGE models try to account for *deep downturns* and *disasters*. Curdia, Del Negro, and Greenwald (2014) estimate the Smets & Wouters (2007) model, assuming Student's *t*-distributed shocks. They find that the fit of the model improves and rare deep downturns become more relevant (see also Fernandez-Villaverde & Levintal, 2018, for a DSGE model with exogenous time-varying rare disaster risk). A similar strategy is employed to Canzoneri et al. (2016) to allow the effects of fiscal policies to change over time and get state-dependent fiscal multipliers higher than one in recessions.

3.4.1 Taking Stock of New DSGE Developments

The new generation of DSGE models tries to address some of the problems mentioned in the previous section. But do post-crisis DSGE models go beyond the intrinsic limits of such an approach and provide a satisfactory account of macroeconomics dynamics? We maintain that the answer is definitely *negative*.

The major advance of the new class of models is the recognition that agents can be heterogeneous in terms of their rationality, consumption preferences (patient vs. impatient), incomes, and so on. However, DSGE models 2.0 can handle only rough forms of heterogeneity and they still do not contemplate direct interactions among agents. Without interactions, they just scratch the surface of the impact of credit and finance on real economic dynamics without explicitly modeling the behaviour of banks (e.g. endogenous risk-taking), network dynamics, financial contagion, the emergence of bankruptcy chains, and the implications of endogenous money. A complex machinery is built just to introduce into the model a new epicycle: exogenous credit shocks.

Similar remarks apply to the other directions of 'advancements'. So, bounded rationality is introduced in homeopathic quantities in order to get quasi-Rational Expectations equilibrium models (Caverzasi & Russo, 2018) with just marginally improved empirical performance. But one can't be a little bit pregnant! The impact of bounded rationality, à la Simon (1959), on macroeconomic dynamics can be pervasive well beyond what can be accounted for by DSGE (see the discussion later in the Element).

Similarly, DSGE models superficially appear able to face both mild and deep downturns, but they in fact only assume them, increasing the degrees of freedom of the models. Indeed, business cycles are still triggered by exogenous shocks, which come from an ad hoc fat-tailed distribution or they are assumed to have massive negative effects.[25] More generally, no DSGE model has ever tried to jointly account for the endogenous emergence of long-run economic growth and business cycles punctuated by deep downturns. Regarding that, the plea of Solow (2005) is still unanswered.

Summing up, we suggest that the recent developments in the DSGE camp are just patches added to a torn cloth. But how many patches can one add before trashing it? For instance, Lindé, Smets, and Wouters (2016), after having expanded the benchmark DSGE model to account for the zero-lower bound, non-Gaussian shocks, and the financial accelerator, conclude that such extensions 'do not suffice to address some of the major policy challenges associated with the use of non-standard monetary policy and macroprudential policies'.[26] More radically, we do think, using Kirman's expression, that the emperor is still naked:[27] DSGE models are simply *post-real* (Romer, 2016). Additional patches are a waste of intellectual (and economic) resources that pushes macroeconomics deeper and deeper into a 'Fantasyland' (Caballero, 2010).

Macroeconomics, we shall argue, should be built on very different grounds based on an understanding of the foundations of complex evolving systems. In the construction of that macroeconomics, evolutionary economics and agent-based computational models represent core building blocks. We present such an alternative paradigm in the rest of this Element.

4 Macroeconomic Agent-Based Models

Agent-based computational economics (ACE) can be defined as the computational study of economies thought of as complex evolving systems (Tesfatsion, 2006; although in fact, Nelson & Winter, 1982 have been the genuine contemporary root of evolutionary ACE, before anyone called them that).

Contrary to DSGE models, and indeed to many other models in economics, ACE provides an alternative methodology to build macroeconomic models

---

[25] Fagiolo, Napoletano, and Roventini (2008) find that GDP growth rates distributions are well proxied by double exponential densities, which dominate both Student's t and Levy-stable distributions. In light of such results, the choice of Curdia, Del Negro, and Greenwald (2014) to drawn shocks from a Student's t distribution is not only ad hoc, but not supported by any empirical evidence.

[26] Lindé, Smets, and Wouters (2016) also conclude that more non-linearities and heterogeneity are required to satisfactory account for default risk, liquidity dynamics, bank runs, as well as to study the interactions between monetary and macroprudential policies.

[27] For a germane discussion about the general equilibrium model, see the classic Kirman (1989).

from the bottom up with sound microfoundations based on realistic assumptions as far as agent behaviours and interactions are concerned, where *realistic* here means rooted in the actual empirical micro-economic evidence (Simon, 1977; Kirman, 2016). The state of economics discipline nowadays is such that it is already subversive in its view that in modeling exercises agents should have the same information as do the economists modeling the economy.

Needless to say, such an epistemological prescription is a progressive step vis-à-vis the idea that theorists, *irrespective of the information they have*, must know as much as God – take or leave some stochastic noise – and agents must know as much as the theorists (or better, theologians and God). However, such a methodology is not enough. First, it is bizarre to think of any isomophism between the knowledge embodied in the observer and that embodied in the object of observation: it is like saying that ants or bees must know as much as the student of anthills and beehives! Second, in actual fact human agents behave according to rules, routines and heuristics which have little to do with either the 'Olympic rationality' or even the 'bounded' one (Gigerenzer, 2007; Gigerenzer & Brighton, 2009; Dosi, Faillo, & Marengo, 2018). The big challenge here, largely still unexplored, concerns the regularities on what people, *and especially organisations* do, concerning for example pricing, investment rules, R&D, hiring and firing, and so on. Half a century ago, we knew much more on mark-up pricing, scrapping and expansionary investment, and more, because there were micro inquiries asking firms 'what do you actually do ...' (more on that in Dosi, 2023, chapter 8). This is mostly over, because at least since the 1980s, the conflict between evidence and theory was definitely resolved: theory is right, evidence must be wrong (or at least well massaged)![28] With that, for example, no responsible advisor would suggest a PhD student to undertake case studies, and no research grant would be requested, on the subject. However, for ABMs all this evidence is the crucial micro behavioural foundation, compared to which current 'calibration exercises'[29] look frankly pathetic.

All this regarding *behaviours*. Another crucial tenet concerns *interactions*.

The ABM, evolutionary, methodology is prone to build whatever macro edifice, whenever possible, upon actual micro interactions. They concern what happens *within organisations* – a subject beyond the scope of this

---

[28] Machlup (1952) crystal-clearly summarises such epistemology: 'When there is an apparent conflict between observations and the theory they are supposed to test, the observations can usually be disqualified as of uncertain reliability; and where this will not do, the conflict can usually be reconciled by means of auxiliary hypotheses.'

[29] Recall that in the presence of flat likelihood functions as those typically associated to the DSGE model, Bayesian estimation simply reduce to a sophisticated calibration exercise. More on that in Section 3.

Element – and *across organisations and individuals*, that is, the *blurred set of markets and networks*. Admittedly, one is very far from any comprehensive understanding of 'how the market works', basically for the same (bogus) reasons as earlier: if one can prove the existence of some market fixed point, why should one bother to show how particularly market mechanics lead there? And, again here, ABMs badly need the evidence on the specific institutional architecture of interactions and their outcomes. Kirman and Vriend (2001) and Kirman (2010a) offer vivid illustrations of the importance of particular institutional set-ups (see also Dosi, 2023, chapter 8).

Fully fledged ABMs require also full-fledged markets. For example, one explores within the K+S family labour markets in Dosi et al. (2017, 2018b). Other exercises on the market have been undertaken by Alan Kirman and colleagues (see chapter 8 of Dosi, 2023).

Short of that, much more concise (and more blackboxed) representations come from network theory (e.g., Albert & Barabasi, 2002) and models of social interactions (e.g., Brock & Durlauf, 2001) which, however, move away from trivial interaction patterns, such as those often implied by game-theoretic frameworks. This together with evidence on persistent heterogeneity and turbulence characterising markets and economies focus the investigation on out-of-equilibrium dynamics endogenously fuelled by the interactions among heterogenous agents.

All those building blocks are more than sufficient to yield the properties of *complex environments*. But what about *evolution*? Basically, that means the *emergence of novelty* entailing, in the economists' jargon, steady changes in the 'fundamentals', and econometrically ubiquitous 'structural breaks'; that is, new technologies, new products, new organisational forms, new behaviours, etc;[30] emerging at some point along the arrow of time, which were not those from the start. Formally, all this may well be captured by *endogenous* dynamics on the 'fundamentals' of the economy. Or, better still, an ever-expanding dimensionality of the state-space and its dynamics (more in Dosi & Winter, 2002 and Dosi & Virgillito, 2017).

4.1 The Basics

Every macroeconomic ABM typically possesses the following structure. There is a population – or a set of populations – of heterogenous agents (e.g., consumers, firms, banks), possibly hierarchically organised, whose size may change or not in time. The evolution of the system is observed in discrete time

---

[30] On a not very long time scale, one should also consider the new physical and social landscapes emerging from the impact of climate change. In an agent-based framework, see Lamperti et al. (2018, 2020).

steps, $t = 1, 2, \ldots$. Time steps may be days, quarters, years, and so on. At each t, every agent i is characterised by a finite number of microeconomic variables $\underline{x}_{i,t}$ which may change across time (e.g., production, consumption, wealth) and by a vector of microeconomic parameters $\underline{\theta}_i$ (e.g., mark-ups, propensity to consume). In turn, the economy may be well characterised by some macroeconomic (fixed) parameters Θ (even mimicking policy like tax rates, the Basel capital requirements, etc.).

Given some initial conditions $\underline{x}_{i,0}$ (e.g., wealth, technology) and a choice for micro and macro parameters, at each time step, one or more agents are chosen to update their microeconomic variables. This may happen randomly or can be triggered by the state of the system itself. Agents picked to perform the updating stage might collect their available information (or not) about the current and past states (i.e., micro-economic variables) of a subset of other agents, typically those they directly interact with. They typically use their knowledge about their own history, their local environment, as well as, possibly, the (limited) information they can gather about the state of the whole economy, and feed them into their heuristics, routines, and other algorithmic behavioural rules. Interactions occur within the population of heterogenous agents. Interactions can involve different agents of the same type (e.g., firms from the same industry) or entities from different types (e.g., trading relationship between firms and consumers in the good market). Such a stream of interactions leads to the emergence of a multi-layer network structure that endogenously evolves over time. At the same time, in truly evolutionary environments, technologies, organisations, behaviours, and markets collectively co-evolve.

After the updating round has taken place, a new set of microeconomic variables is fed into the economy for the next-step iteration: aggregate variables $\underline{X}_t$ are computed by simply summing up or averaging individual characteristics. Once again, the definitions of aggregate variables closely follow those of statistical aggregates (i.e., GDP, unemployment).

4.2 Emergence and Validation

The stochastic components possibly present in decision rules, expectations, and interactions in turn requires that the dynamics of micro and macro variables ought to be typically described by some stochastic processes. The *non-linearities* which are typically present in the dynamics of agent-based systems make it hard to analytically derive closed-form properties of their laws of motion. Together, their stochastic version might well entail instances of non-ergodicity. This suggests that the researcher must often resort to computer simulations in order to analyse the behaviour of the ABM at hand. And even there, the detection of such 'laws of motion' is no simple matter, as history counts, even in the longer term.

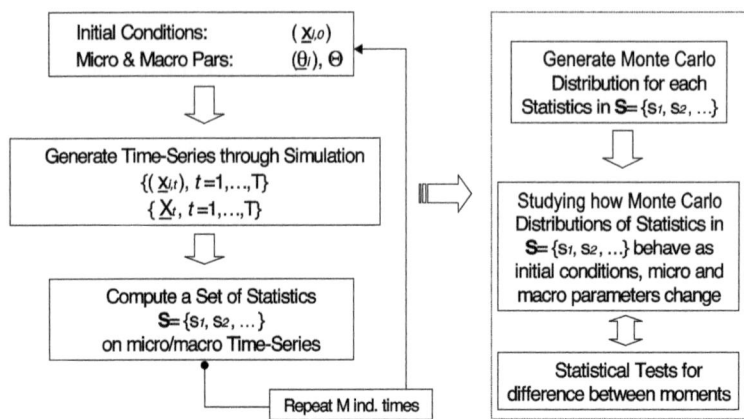

Figure 1 A schematic procedure for studying the output of an agent-based model.
Source: Fagiolo and Roventini (2012).

How are simulations carried out in agent-based economics? A possible procedure that can be implemented to study the output of simulation is synthetically depicted in Figure 1. Given some choice for initial conditions, micro and macro parameters, the system can be run until it reaches some stable behaviour (i.e., for at least $T > T^*$ time steps). Suppose one is interested in a set $S = s1, s2, \ldots$ of statistics to be computed on micro and macro simulated variables (e.g. average GDP growth rates, unemployment rates, distributions of firm sizes, productivities and profitabilities). Given the stochastic nature of the process, each run will output a different value for the statistics of interest. Therefore, after having produced M independent runs, which we refer to as Monte Carlo simulations, one has a distribution for each statistic containing M observations, which can be summarised by computing its moments. Recall, however, that moments will depend *at least* on the choice made for initial conditions and parameters (and not only on them if history really counts). By exploring a sufficiently large number of points in the space where initial conditions and parameters are allowed to vary, computing the moments of the statistics of interest at each point, and by assessing how moments depend on parameters, one might get a quite deep descriptive knowledge of the behaviour of the system (see Figure 1).

Simulation exercises allow one then to study long-run statistical distributions, patterns, and emergent properties of micro and macro dynamics. For instance, a macro agent-based model can endogenously generate apparently ordered patterns of growth together with business cycles and deep crises. In that ABMs provide a direct answer to Solow and Stiglitz's plea for macroeconomic models that can jointly account for long-run trajectories, short-run fluctuations, and deep downturns (see Section 1). At the same time, such models deliver a wealth of emergent properties ranging from macroeconomic relationships such as the Okun and Phillips curves to microeconomic distributions of, for example, firm size and growth rates, and so on. Moreover, as with every complex system, after crossing some critical threshold or tipping point the economy can self-organise along a different statistical path. This allows one to straightforwardly study phenomena like hysteresis in unemployment and GDP, systemic risk in credit, and financial markets, climate-change tipping points, and others.

More generally, the very structure of ABMs naturally allows one to take the model to the data and validate it against observed real-world observations. Most ABMs follow what has been called an *indirect calibration approach* (Windrum & Moneta, 2007; Fagiolo et al. 2017) which indeed represents also a powerful form of validation: the models are required to match a possibly wide set of micro and macro empirical regularities. An impressive list of micro and macro stylized facts jointly accounted by macro agent-based models is presented in Section 6; more in Haldane and Turrell (2019), Dosi et al. (2016a) and Dosi et al. (2020) among others. For instance, at the macro level, ABMs are able to match the relative volatility and comovements between GDP and different macroeconomic variables, the interactions between real, credit, and financial aggregates (including the emergence of deep banking crises), fat-tailed GDP growth-rate distributions, and so on. At the microeconomic level, macro agent-based models are able to reproduce firm size and growth rate distributions, heterogeneity and persistent differentials among firm productivity, lumpy investment patterns, and so on.

We do consider the *ability of ABMs to jointly account for a huge ensemble of both micro and macro stylised facts under a wide range of parameterisations as the primary validation of their strength and robustness.* In fact, it is relatively easy to 'prove' any model, no matter how far-fetched, concerning any one empirical regularity, in violation of all the rest we know about that particular phenomenon. So, for example, in the Middle Ages, there were astronomical theories apparently quite apt to 'explain' the day and the night in terms of God opening and closing the curtains of the universe. The analogy with DSGE models is striking indeed! However, the ABM perspective has accepted also such an epistemologically twisted comparative challenge and has made much progress even in terms of *validation* against a single time-series. A detailed survey with the most recent developments is provided in Fagiolo, Guerini, Lamperti et al. (2017).

On the 'input side', that is, modelling assumptions about individual 'behaviours' and interactions have been refined on laboratory experiments (Hommes, 2013; Anufriev, Bao, & Tuinstra, 2016), business practices (Dawid et al. 2019) and, more generally, microeconomic empirical evidence (Dosi et al., 2016a).[31] ABMs can also be validated on the output side, by explaining the space of parameters and initial conditions in terms of the range of values which allow the model to replicate the stylised facts of interest. For instance, Barde (2016) and Lamperti (2018) attempt to validate the output of agent-based models according to the replication of time-series dynamics, while Guerini and Moneta (2017) explore how a macro ABM matches the apparent causal relations in the data. Some works estimate ABMs via indirect inference (see e.g. Alfarano, Lux, & Wagner, 2005; Winker, Gilli, & Jeleskovic, 2007; Grazzini, Richiardi, & Sellad, 2013; Grazzini & Richiardi, 2015) or Bayesian methods (Delli Gatti & Grazzini, 2020; Grazzini, Richiardi, & Tsionas, 2017). Finally, a new strand of research assesses the forecasting capabilities of ABMs vis-à-vis DSGE and VAR models (Poledna et al., 2023).

In any case, there is a *fundamental distinction*, often neglected by economists, *between explanation and forecasting*. One may well use clearly wrong theories in order to predict especially in the short term, and they might well be the ground for powerful heuristics for decision. Agent-based models of the K+S kind are primarily there with the ambition to *explain*. Together, they are also instrumental in showing the power of *wrong models of* prediction as robust guidance to behaviours in complex evolving environments. So in Dosi et al. (2020a), for example, one shows that the prediction rule 'tomorrow will be likely today' turns out to be a much more effective guidance for individual behaviours in complex and changing worlds than any more sophisticated inferential rule.

No matter the empirical validation procedures actually employed, an important domain of analysis regards the *sensitivity* of the model to parameter changes through different methods including Kriging meta-modeling (Salle & Yıldızoğlu, 2014; Dosi, Pereira, & Virgillito, 2017; Dosi et al., 2018a, 2018b; Bargigli et al., 2020) and machine-learning surrogates (Lamperti, Roventini, & Sani, 2018). Such methodologies provide detailed sensitivity analyses of macro ABMs, allowing one to get a quite deep descriptive knowledge of the behaviour of the system, even concerning variables far from crucial for the general interpretative power of ABMs themselves. In this respect, however, note that, contrary to common wisdom, the most 'important' variables, whatever it means in a system rich of inter-relatedness, are those which are most *insensitive* to changes in parameterisations. What counts is

---

[31] The increasing supply of big data is likely to considerably improve the input validation of agent-based models. Incidentally, this is not going to apply to representative-agent DSGE models.

primarily their presence or absence. This is the case, for example, of an innovation process of whatever kind, or a mechanism of demand generation, or a fiscal policy, again of whatever kind.

4.3 Policy Analysis

If empirically sound, agent-based models represent a very powerful device able to address policy questions under more realistic, flexible, and modular set-ups. Indeed, in contrast to DSGE models, they do not impose any strong theoretical consistency requirements (e.g., equilibrium, representative individual assumptions, rational expectations) and allow for behavioural assumptions which can be replaced in a modular way, without impairing the analysis of the model.[32] Moreover, as already mentioned earlier, agent-based models are able to jointly match a rich ensemble of macro and micro empirical regularities. This is a major advantage of ABMs vis-à-vis, for example, DSGE ones, which are typically built – in order to retain analytical solvability – to explain very few macro-stylised facts, and cannot replicate by construction any micro empirical regularities, given their representative-agent assumption.

But how can one actually conduct policy experiments in ABMs? In a very natural way, indeed. Take again the procedure for ABM descriptive analysis outlined in Figure 1. Micro and macro parameters can be designed in such a way to mimic real-world key policy variables like tax rates, subsidies, and others. Moreover, initial conditions might play a relevant role (somewhat equivalent to initial endowments in standard models) and describe different distributional set-ups concerning, for example, incomes or technologies. In addition, interaction and behavioural rules employed by economic agents can be easily devised so as to represent alternative institutional, market, or industry set-ups. Since all these elements can be freely interchanged, one can investigate a huge number of alternative policy experiments and rules, the consequences of which can be assessed either qualitatively or quantitatively (e.g., by running standard statistical tests on the distributions of the statistics in S). For example, one might statistically test whether the effect on the moments of the individual consumption distribution will be changed (and if so, by how much) by a percentage change in any given consumption tax rate. Most importantly, all this might be done while preserving the ability of the model to replicate existing macroeconomic stylized facts, as well as microeconomic empirical regularities, which by construction cannot be matched by DSGE models.

---

[32] According to Moss (2008) one advantage of ABMs is that they also allow policymakers to be involved in the development of the model to be employed for policy evaluations.

4.4 Conclusions

The number of macroeconomic agent-based models has steadily increased in the last decades, and this trend received a new impulse after the Great Recession uncovered many weaknesses of DSGE models. For instance, in their survey Dawid and Delli Gatti (2018) discuss eight families of macroeconomic agent-based models: the model of Ashraf, Gershman, and Howitt (2017), the Ancona–Milano approach (Delli Gatti et al., 2005; Assenza, Delli Gatti, & Grazzini, 2015), the Eurace@Unibi model (Dawid et al., 2014a; Dawid, Harting, & Neugart, 2014b, 2018), the Eurace simulator developed in Genoa (Cincotti, Raberto, & Teglio, 2010; Raberto et al., 2019; Teglio et al., 2019), the JAMEL model (Salle & Seppecher, 2018; Seppecher, 2018), the Keynes meeting Schumpeter model (Dosi, Fagiolo, & Roventini, 2010), the LAGOM model (Mandel, Jaeger, Fuerst et al., 2010; Wolf, Furst, Mandel et al., 2013), and the model developed by Lengnick (2013). The list is not completely exhaustive. Among a burgeoning line of research, one should consider, for instance, the stock-flow consistent model by Caiani et al. (2016), and the multi-industry models developed independently by Ciarli et al. (2019), Dosi, Roventini, and Russo (2019, 2020), and Poledna et al. (2023).

The surveys of Fagiolo and Roventini (2012, 2017), Napoletano (2018), and Dawid and Delli Gatti (2018) show how macroeconomic agent-based models can succesfully address fiscal policy, monetary policy, macroprudential policy, labour-market governance, regional and cohesion policies, innovation and industrial policies, climate-change policies,[33] and different combinations of such public interventions. In that, ABMs are a valuable tool in the model portfolio available for policymakers as discussed by Haldane and Turrell (2019). An overview of such models is beyond the scope of the Element. On the contrary, in the next section, we will introduce the family of Keynes meeting Schumpeter models refining upon Dosi, Fagiolo, and Roventini (2010), which can be considered our workhorse ABM accounting for macro and micro dynamics, as well as for testing the impact of different combinations of microeconomic and macroeconomic policies.

5 The Schumpeter Meeting Keynes Model

The Schumpeter meeting Keynes (K+S) family of agent-based models (Dosi, Fagiolo & Roventini 2010; Dosi et al. 2013, 2015, 2017, 2018a, 2019, 2020a) is able to jointly account for endogenous growth and business fluctuations

---

[33] For a survey of agent-based models studying climate change issues, see Balint et al. (2017).

punctuated by major crises.[34] In that, it responds to the pleas of Solow (2005) and Stiglitz (2011) to design models that knit together short- and long-run dynamics, as well as are able to account for rare deep downturns. Beyond that, the K+S model reproduces a rich list of macro and micro stylised facts and it can be employed as a laboratory to test the short- and long-run impact of different ensembles of innovation, industrial, fiscal, and monetary policies.

Rooted in the evolutionary (Nelson & Winter, 1982, see also Dosi et al., 1988) and agent-based (cf. Tesfatsion, 2006) perspectives, the K+S model addresses five major, interrelated, questions. First, it investigates the processes by which technological innovations affect macro variables such as unemployment rates and, in the longer term, output growth rates.

Together with this 'Schumpeterian' question, second, we ask how such endogenous changes in the 'fundamentals' of the economy interact with demand conditions. This is a basic 'Keynesian' question. How does aggregate demand modulate the diffusion and the macro impact of technological innovations? And, conversely, how does it affect, if at all, the amount of search and the degree of exploitation of innovation opportunities themselves?

Third, we explore long-term effects of demand conditions. Is the long-term growth just driven by changes in the technological 'fundamentals'? Or, can variations in aggregate demand influence future dynamics?

Four, the K+S model investigates the interactions between the real and financial sides of the economy, thus reproducing the Minskian features of business cycles (Minsky, 1986) and the endogenous emergence of banking crises.

Fifth, it allows the exploitation of the properties and impact of different arrangements in the institutions governing labour relations, including the way labour markets operate, and wages are set.

Sixth, it allows the study of the intrinsic duality of technological change with its labour-shedding effect via productivity improvements, on the one side, and the job-creating effect via the introduction of new products, on the other.

The fully fledged version of the K+S model describes an economy with heterogeneous firms – belonging either to a capital- or consumption-good industry – banks, a labour force, a central bank, and a government (see Figure 2). Innovation and imitation routines performed by capital-goods firms investing in R&D drive the process of technical change, resulting in cheaper and far more productive machines sold to the consumption-goods sector. The latter firms produce (in the baseline version of the model) a homogeneous final good and may use external financing from the banking sector if their internal resources do not cover production and investment expenses. Both firms and

---

[34] This section draws on Dosi, Fagiolo, & Roventini (2010), Dosi et al. (2016a) and Dosi et al. (2020b).

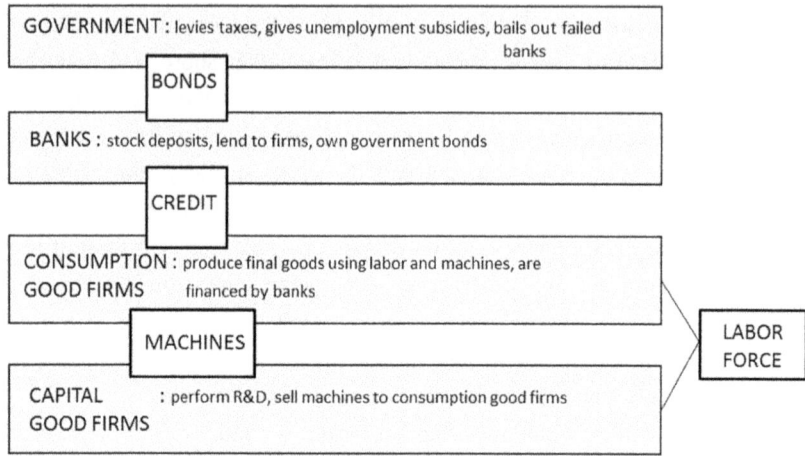

Figure 2 A schematic representation of the Schumpeter meeting Keynes (K+S) model.

banks can go bankrupt if their net worth becomes negative, possibly triggering a crisis. The government fixes taxes and unemployment subsidy rates and bails out bankrupted banks. The central bank sets the baseline interest rate for the economy.

In what follows, we present the basic K+S model and its credit-market and labour-market extensions. The empirical validation of the model will be reported in Section 6. Finally, the policy experiments will be presented in Section 7.

5.1 The Timeline of Events

As already mentioned, our simple economy is composed of a machine-producing sector made of F_1 firms (denoted by the subscript i), a consumption-good sector made of F_2 firms (denoted by the subscript j), L^S consumers/workers, and a public sector. Before accurately describing the K+S model (Dosi, Fagiolo, & Roventini, 2010), we briefly provide the timeline of events occurring in each time step (t).

1. Machine-tool firms perform R&D trying to discover new products and more efficient production techniques and to imitate the technology and the products of their competitors.
2. Capital-good firms advertise their machines with consumption-good producers.
3. Consumption-good firms decide how much to produce and invest. If investment is positive, consumption-good firms choose their supplier and send

their orders, for their planned expansion, and, possibly, also to replace some older equipments.
4. In both industries firms hire workers according to their production plans and start producing.
5. Imperfectly competitive consumption-good market opens. The market shares of firms evolve according to their 'competitiveness' based on prices and possibly other variables such as any unfilled demand.
6. Entry and exit take places. In both sectors firms with near-zero market shares and negative net liquid assets are eschewed from the two industries and replaced by new firms.
7. Machines ordered at the beginning of the period are delivered and become part of the capital stock at time $t + 1$.

At the end of each time step, aggregate variables (e.g. GDP, investment, employment) are computed, summing over the corresponding microeconomic variables.

Let us now turn to a more detailed description of the model and of the agents' behaviours, which – to repeat – we try to keep as close as we can to what we know they actually do as distinct from what they ought to do under more perfect informational circumstances.

5.2 The Capital-Good Industry

The technology of a capital-good firm is (A_i^τ, B_i^τ), where the former coefficient stands for the labour productivity of the machine-tool manufactured by i for the consumption-good industry (a rough measure of producer quality), while the latter coefficient is the labour productivity of the production technique employed by firm i itself. The positive integer τ denotes the current technology vintage. Given the monetary wage w, the unit cost of production of capital-good firms is:

$$c_i(t) = \frac{w(t)}{B_i^\tau}. \tag{1}$$

With a fixed mark-up ($\mu_1 > 0$) pricing rule,[35] prices (p_i) are defined as:

$$p_i(t) = (1 + \mu_1)c_i(t). \tag{2}$$

The unit labour cost of production in the consumption-good sector associated with each machine of vintage τ, produced by firm i is:

$$c(A_i^\tau, t) = \frac{w(t)}{A_i^\tau}.$$

---
[35] See the directions of the behavioural evidence in Dosi (2023) and also Fabiani et al. (2006) on European firms: prices are generally set according to mark-up rules.

Firms in the capital-good industry 'adaptively' strive to increase their market shares and their profits trying to improve their technology both via innovation and imitation. Both are costly processes: firms invest in R&D a fraction of their past sales (S_i):

$$RD_i(t) = vS_i(t-1), \qquad (3)$$

with $0 < v < 1$. R&D expenditures are employed to hire researchers paying the market wage $w(t)$.[36] Firms split their R&D efforts between innovation (*IN*) and imitation (*IM*) according to the parameter $\xi \in [0,1]$:

$$IN_i(t) = \xi RD_i(t),$$
$$IM_i(t) = (1-\xi)RD_i(t).$$

We model innovation as a two-step process. The first one determines whether a firm obtains or not an access to innovation – irrespectively of whether it is ultimately a success or a failure – through a draw from a Bernoulli distribution, whose parameter $\theta_i^{in}(t)$ is given by:

$$\theta_i^{in}(t) = 1 - e^{-\zeta_1 IN_i(t)}, \qquad (4)$$

with $0 < \zeta_1 \leq 1$ capturing *firms' search capabilities*. Note that according to (4), there are some scale-related returns to R&D investment: access to innovative discoveries is more likely if a firm puts more resources into R&D. If a firm innovates, it may draw a new machine embodying technology (A_i^{in}, B_i^{in}) according to:

$$A_i^{in}(t) = A_i(t)(1 + x_i^A(t)),$$
$$B_i^{in}(t) = B_i(t)(1 + x_i^B(t)),$$

where x_i^A and x_i^B are two independent draws from a Beta(α_1, β_1) distribution over the support $[\underline{x}_1, \bar{x}_1]$ with $\underline{x}_1$ belonging to the interval $[-1, 0]$ and $\bar{x}_1$ to $[0,1]$. Note that the notional possibilities of technological advance – namely *technological opportunities* (Dosi, 2023) – are captured by the support of the Beta distribution and by its shape. So, for example, with low opportunities the largest probability density falls over 'failed' innovations – that is, potential capital goods which are 'worse' in terms of costs and performances than those already produced by the searching firm. Conversely, under a condition of

---

[36] In the following, we assume all capital-producing firms to be identical in their R&D propensity. This is not too far from reality: R&D intensities are largely sector specific and associated with the *sector-wide* nature of innovative opportunities and modes of innovative search (more in Pavitt, 1984; Klevorick et al., 1995; Dosi, 2023).

rich opportunities, innovations which dominate incumbent technologies will be drawn with high probability. As we shall show later in the Element, a crucial role of 'Schumpeterian' technology policies is precisely to influence opportunities and micro capabilities.

Like innovation search, imitation follows a two-step procedure. The possibilities of accessing imitation come from sampling a Bernoulli, $(\theta_i^{im}(t))$:

$$\theta_i^{im}(t) = 1 - e^{-\zeta_2 IM_i(t)}, \tag{5}$$

with $0 < \zeta_2 \leqslant 1$. Firms accessing the second stage are able to copy the technology of one of the competitors (A_i^{im}, B_i^{im}). We assume that firms are more likely to imitate competitors with similar technologies and we use a Euclidean metric to compute the technological distance between every pair of firms to weight imitation probabilities. Such *appropriability conditions* stem from the tacit nature of knowledge embodied in the technology, even in the presence of explicit intellectual properties rights (which, however, can be easily modeled in our framework).

All firms which draw a potential innovation or imitation have to put it on production or keep producing the incumbent generation of machines. Comparing the technology competing for adoption, firms choose to manufacture the machine characterised by the best trade-off between price and efficiency. More specifically, knowing that consumption-good firms invest following a payback period routine (see Section 5.3), capital-good firms select the machine to produce according to the following rule:

$$\min \left[p_i^h(t) + bc^h(A_i^h, t) \right], \quad h = \tau, in, im, \tag{6}$$

where b is a positive payback period parameter (see Eq. 10). Once the type of machine is chosen, we capture the imperfect information pervading the market, assuming that each firm sends a 'brochure' with the price and the productivity of its offered machines to both its historical (HC_i) clients and to a random sample of potential new customers (NC_i), whose size is proportional to HC_i (i.e., $NC_i(t) = \gamma HC_i(t)$, with $0 < \gamma < 1$).

5.3 The Consumption-Good Industry

Consumption-good firms produce a homogenous goods using capital (i.e. their stock of machines) and labour under constant returns to scale. Firms plan their production (Q_j) according to adaptive demand expectations (D_j^e):

$$D_j^e(t) = f(D_j(t-1), D_j(t-2), \ldots, D_j(t-h)), \tag{7}$$

where $D_j(t-1)$ is the demand actually faced by firm j at time $t-1$ (h positive integer).[37] The desired level of production (Q_j^d) depends on the expected demand as well as on the desired inventories (N_j^d) and the actual stock of inventories (N_j):

$$Q_j^d(t) = D_j^e(t) + N_j^d(t) - N_j(t-1), \tag{8}$$

with $N_j^d(t) = \iota D_j^e(t), \iota \in [0,1]$. The output of consumption-good firms is constrained by their capital stock (K_j). If the desired capital stock (K_j^d) – computed as a function of the desired level of production – is higher than the current capital stock, firms invest (EI_j^d) in order to expand their production capacity:[38]

$$EI_j^d(t) = K_j^d(t) - K_j(t). \tag{9}$$

The capital stock of each firm is obviously composed of heterogenous vintages of machines with different productivity. We define $\Xi_j(t)$ as the set of all vintages of machine-tools belonging to firm j at time t. Firms scrap machines following a payback period routine. Consequently, technical change and equipment prices influence the replacement decisions of consumption-good firms.[39] More specifically, firm j replaces machine $A_i^\tau \in \Xi_j(t)$ according to its technology obsolescence as well as the price of new machines:

$$RS_j(t) = \left\{ A_i^\tau \in \Xi_j(t) : \frac{p^*(t)}{c(A_{i,\tau},t) - c^*(t)} \leq b \right\}, \tag{10}$$

where p^* and c^* are the price and unit cost of production upon the new machines. Firms compute their replacement investment by summing up the number of old machine-tools, satisfying Eq. 10. Moreover, they also scrap the machines older than η periods (with η being a positive integer).

Consumption-good firms choose their capital-good supplier by comparing the price and productivity of the currently manufactured machine-tools they are aware of. As we mentioned earlier (see Section 5.2), the capital-good market

---

[37] For maximum simplicity, we often use the rule $D_j^e(t) = D_j(t-1)$. In Dosi, Fagiolo, and Roventini (2006) and in Dosi et al. (2020a) we check the robustness of the assumption employing also more sophisticated expectation-formation rules. As already mentioned, we found that increasing the computational capabilities and information availability, *at most*, does *not* affect system dynamics. However, most often it makes individual and macro fates, *worse off*. The reason is simple indeed: attempts to interpret a complex and non-stationary world with stationary lenses are, at best, futile or more generally harmful and self-defeating (more in Dosi, 2023, and, on the general point of expectations, Gigerenzer & Brighton, 2009).

[38] We assume in our model so far that, in any given period, firm capital growth rates cannot exceed a fixed maximum threshold consistent with the maximum capital growth rates found in the empirical literature on firm investment patterns (e.g. Doms & Dunne, 1998).

[39] This is in line with a large body of empirical analyses (e.g., Feldstein & Foot, 1971; Eisner, 1972; Goolsbee, 1998) showing that replacement investment is typically not proportional to the capital stock.

is systematically characterised by imperfect information. This implies that consumption-good firms compare 'brochures' describing the characteristics of machines only from a subset of equipment suppliers. Firms then choose the machines with the lowest price and unit cost of production (i.e., $p_i(t) + bc(A_i^\tau, t)$) and send their orders to the corresponding machine manufacturer. Machine production is a time-consuming process: capital-good firms deliver the ordered machine-tools at the end of the period.[40] Gross investment of each firm (I_j) is the sum of expansion and replacement investment. Pooling the investment of all consumption-good firms, one gets aggregate investment (I).

Consumption-good firms have to finance their investments, as well as their production, as they advance worker wages. In line with any empirical observation and also a growing number of theoretical and empirical papers (e.g. Stiglitz & Weiss, 1992; Greenwald & Stiglitz, 1993a; Hubbard, 1998), we assume imperfect capital markets. This implies that the financial structure of firms matters (external funds are more expensive than internal ones) and firms may be credit rationed. More specifically, consumption-good firms finance production using their stock of liquid assets (NW_j). If liquid assets do not fully cover production costs, firms borrow the remaining part, paying an interest rate r up to a maximum debt/sales ratio of Λ. Only firms that are not production-rationed can try to fulfill their investment plans by employing their residual stock of liquid assets first and then their residual borrowing capacity.[41]

Given their current stock of machines, consumption-good firms compute average productivity (π_j) and unit cost of production (c_j). Prices are set applying a variable mark-up (μ_j) on unit costs of production:

$$p_j(t) = (1 + \mu_j(t))c_j(t). \tag{11}$$

Mark-up variations are regulated by the evolution of firm market shares (f_j):[42]

$$\mu_j(t) = \mu_j(t-1)\left(1 + \upsilon \frac{f_j(t-1) - f_j(t-2)}{f_j(t-2)}\right), \tag{12}$$

with $0 \leqslant \upsilon \leqslant 1$.

The consumption-good market too is characterised by imperfect information (antecedents in the same vein are Phelps and Winter, 1970; Klemperer, 1987; Farrel & Shapiro, 1988; see also the empirical literature on consumers'

---

[40] Among the empirical literature investigating the presence of gestation-lag effects in firm investment expenditures, see e.g. Del Boca et al. (2008).
[41] If investment plans cannot be fully realized, firms give priority to capital stock expansion, as compared to the substitution of old machines.
[42] This is close to the spirit of 'customer market' models originated by the seminal work of Phelps and Winter (1970). See also Klemperer (1995) for a survey and the exploration of some important macro implications by Greenwald and Stiglitz (2003).

imperfect price knowledge surveyed in Rotemberg, 2008). This implies that consumers do not instantaneously switch to products made by more competitive firms. However, prices are clearly one of the key determinants of firms' *competitiveness* (E_j). The other component is the level of unfilled demand (l_j) inherited from the previous period:

$$E_j(t) = -\omega_1 p_j(t) - \omega_2 l_j(t), \qquad (13)$$

where $\omega_{1,2}$ are positive parameters.[43] Weighting the competitiveness of each consumption-good firm by its past market share (f_j), one can compute the *average competitiveness* of the consumption-good sector:

$$\overline{E}(t) = \sum_{j=1}^{F_2} E_j(t) f_j(t-1).$$

This variable represents also a moving *selection criterion* driving, other things being equal, expansion, contraction, and extinction within the population of firms. We parsimoniously model this market set-up, letting firm market shares evolve according to a 'quasi' replicator dynamics (for antecedents in the evolutionary camp see Metcalfe, 1994a; Silverberg, Dosi, & Orsenigo, 1988):

$$f_j(t) = f_j(t-1)\left(1 + \chi \frac{E_j(t) - \overline{E}(t)}{\overline{E}(t)}\right), \qquad (14)$$

with $\chi > 0$.[44]

The profits (Π_j) of each consumption-good firm reads:

$$\Pi_j(t) = S_j(t) - c_j(t) Q_j(t) - r Deb_j(t),$$

where $S_j(t) = p_j(t) D_j(t)$ and Deb denotes the stock of debt. The investment choices of each firm and its profits determine the evolution of its stock of liquid assets (NW_j):

$$NW_j(t) = NW_j(t-1) + \Pi_j(t) - cI_j(t),$$

where cI_j is the amount of internal funds employed by firm j to finance investment.

---

[43] Recall that consumption-good firms fix production according to their demand expectations, which may differ from actual demand. If the firm produced too much, the inventories pile up, whereas if its production is lower than demand plus inventories, its competitiveness is accordingly reduced.

[44] Strictly speaking, a canonic replicator dynamics evolves on the unit simplex with all entities having positive shares. Equation 14 allows shares to become virtually negative. In that case, the firm is declared dead and market shares are accordingly re-calculated. This is what we mean by a 'quasi-replicator' dynamics. Note that an advantage of such formulation is that it determines at the same time changes in market shares and extinction events.

5.4 Schumpeterian Exit and Entry Dynamics

At the end of each period, we let firms with (quasi) zero market shares or negative net assets die and we allow a new breed of firms to enter the markets. In many of our models, we keep the number of firms fixed, hence any dead firm is replaced by a new one (this simplifying assumption is, however, by no means a necessary one).

In line with the empirical literature on firm entry (Caves, 1998; Bartelsman, Scarpetta, & Schivardi, 2005), we assume that entrants are on average smaller than incumbents, with the stock of capital of new consumption-good firms and the stock of liquid assets of entrants in both sectors being a fraction of the average stocks of the incumbents. More specifically, the stock of capital of a new consumption-good firm is obtained by multiplying the average stock of capital of the incumbents by a random draw from a Uniform distribution with support $[\phi_1, \phi_2], 0 < \phi_1, < \phi_2 \leqslant 1$. In the same manner, the stock of liquid assets of an entrant is computed by multiplying the average stock of liquid assets of the incumbents of the sector by a random variable distributed according to a Uniform distribution with support $[\phi_3, \phi_4], 0 < \phi_3, < \phi_4 \leqslant 1$.

Concerning the technology of entrants, new consumption-good firms select amongst the newest vintages of machines according to the 'brochure mechanism' described earlier. The process- and product-related knowledge of new capital-good firms is again drawn from a Beta distribution, whose shape and support are shifted and 'twisted' according to whether entrants enjoy an advantage or a disadvantage vis-à-vis incumbents. More precisely, the technology of capital-good firms is obtained by applying a coefficient extracted from a Beta(α_2, β_2) distribution to the endogenously evolving technology frontier ($A^{max}(t), B^{max}(t)$), where $A^{max}(t)$ and $B^{max}(t)$ are the best technology available to incumbents. In fact, the distribution of opportunities for entrants versus incumbents is a crucial characteristic of different sectoral *technological regimes* (a particular case of that is the distance from the technological frontier of entrants discussed in Aghion & Howitt, 2007).

5.5 The Labour Market

The labour market is certainly not Walrasian: real wages not claring the market and involuntary unemployment as well as labour rationing are the rules rather than the exceptions. The aggregate labour demand (L^D) is computed by summing up the labour demand of capital- and consumption-good firms. The aggregate supply (L^S) is exogenous and inelastic. Hence aggregate employment (L) is the minimum between L^D and L^S.

The wage rate is determined by institutional and market factors. In the simplest case, which we use in our baseline version, wages are determined at the macro level via indexation mechanisms upon consumption prices and average productivity, on the one hand, and adjustments to unemployment rates, on the other:

$$w(t) = w(t-1) + \left(1 + \psi_1 \frac{\Delta \overline{AB}(t)}{\overline{AB}(t-1)} + \psi_2 \frac{\Delta cpi(t)}{cpi(t-1)} + \psi_3 \frac{\Delta U(t)}{U(t-1)}\right), \quad (15)$$

where $\overline{AB}$ is the average labour productivity, cpi is the consumer price index, and U is the unemployment rate. Variations may be experimented with, mimicking different regimes for the labour market, by changing the system parameters $\psi_{1,2,3}$. However, more adequate representations of different regimes in a genuine ABM spirit are required. We present some promising attempts in Section 5.8. In any case, note that the analogy between Eq. 15 and any form of 'Phillips curve' is only superficial. Indeed, our results hold even if the coefficient on the unemployment term is set to zero. The importance of the relation is in terms of the transmission process from productivity to wages (or the absence thereof).

5.6 Consumption, Taxes, and Public Expenditures

An otherwise black-boxed public sector levies taxes on firm profits and worker wages or on profits only and pays to unemployed workers a subsidy (w^u) that is a fraction of the current market wage (i.e., $w^u(t) = \varphi w(t)$, with $\varphi \in (0,1)$). In fact, taxes and subsidies are the fiscal leverages that contribute to the aggregate demand management regimes (we shall explore this issue in more detail later). Note that a 'zero tax, zero subsidy' scenario is our benchmark for a *pure Schumpeterian regime* of institutional governance (see the experiments in Section 7).

Aggregate consumption (C) is computed by summing up over the income of both employed and unemployed workers:

$$C(t) = w(t)L^D(t) + w^u(L^S - L^D(t)). \quad (16)$$

The model satisfies the standard national account identities: the sum of value added of capital- and consumption goods firms (GDP) equals their aggregate production since in our simplified economy there are no intermediate goods, and that in turn coincides with the sum of aggregate consumption, investment, and change in inventories (ΔN):

$$GDP_t \equiv \sum_{i=1}^{F_1} Q_i(t) + \sum_{j=1}^{F_2} Q_j(t) \equiv C(t) + I(t) + \Delta N(t).$$

The dynamics generated at the micro level by decisions of a multiplicity of heterogenous, adaptive agents and by their interaction mechanisms is the explicit microfoundation of the dynamics for all aggregate variables of interest (e.g. output, investment, employment). However, as the model amply demonstrates, the aggregate properties of the economy do not bear any apparent isomorphism with the micro adjustment rules outlined earlier. Needless to say, a fundamental consequence is also that any 'representative agent' compression of micro heterogeneity is likely to offer a distorted account of both what agents do and the collective outcomes of their actions – more in Dosi (2023), indeed, well in tune with the arguments of Kirman (1992) and Solow (2008).

5.7 The Credit Market Extensions

Building on the initial set-up presented and tested in Dosi, Fagiolo & Roventini (2010), the model has been extended (Dosi et al., 2013, 2015), introducing a credit market populated by heterogenous banks in order to study the possible interplays between the real and financial sectors. Such addition allows us to investigate the role of credit in amplifying and triggering macroeconomic fluctuations, possibly leading to the emergence of bank and sovereign debt crises and deep downturns that could affect the long-run performance of the economy (see Levine, 1997, explicitly opposing Schumpeter's view on that). The credit sector is populated by B heterogenous banks, which gather deposits, distribute loans, and own sovereign bonds. In addition, a central bank now sets the baseline interest rate following a Taylor rule.

Banks are heterogenous in their number of clients (drawn from a Pareto distribution). Credit supply is constrained by capital adequacy requirements inspired by Basel-framework rules. Besides the regulatory limit, we assume that banks maintain a buffer over the regulatory capital level, as indicated by the empirical evidence (BIS, 1999). The size of such buffers evolves strategically in order to offset bank financial fragility along the business cycle, and it is proxied by the ratio between accumulated bad debt (i.e. loans in default) and bank assets (i.e. sum of the stocks of loans, sovereign bonds, and reserves held by the bank), $Bda_{k,t}$. Total credit supply available from bank k at time t therefore is as follows:

$$TC_{k,t} = \frac{NW^b_{k,t-1}}{\tau^b(1 + \beta Bda_{k,t-1})}, \qquad (17)$$

where $\beta > 0$ is a parameter that measures the banks' speed of adjustment to its financial fragility, and τ^b is the macroprudential regulatory parameter. Credit supply therefore decreases in β and τ and is positively affected by banks' equity.

Banks allocate credit across firms by ranking them according to their creditworthiness, proxied by the ratio between firms' past net worth and sales. Loans are granted to firms as long as credit supply is not exhausted. As a consequence, consumption-goods firms may be credit-rationed. Firms' probability to get a loan depends on their credit ranking as well as on the financial health of their bank. Note that the lower performance of other clients improves firms' relative ranking, but also has a negative impact on total credit availability, because firms' defaults weaken the equity of their bank, thus reducing the supply of credit.

We assume that the central bank follows a Taylor rule, which adjusts the interest rate to changes in inflation and, under some revealing policy scenarios, to unemployment, relative to their target levels:

$$r_t = r^T + \gamma_\pi(\pi_t - \pi^T) + \gamma_U(U^T - U_t), \qquad \gamma_\pi > 1, \gamma_U \geq 0, \qquad (18)$$

where π_t is the inflation rate of the period, U_t the unemployment rate, and r^T, π^T, U^T are the target interest, inflation, and unemployment rates, respectively. Banks fix the interest rate on loans by applying a risk premium on the policy rate.

Bank revenues are composed of interests from loans, deposits at the central bank, and sovereign bonds. Gross profits are taxed at the rate tr. Massive loan losses may turn profits negative, reducing the equity of banks and their credit supply. A bank goes bankrupt if firm bankruptcy shocks turn its net worth negative. In such a case, the government steps in and recapitalizes the bank. The public bailout entails a cost ($Gbailout_{t,k}$), equal to the difference between the equity of the failed bank before and after the intervention, which affects the public budget.

Given government tax revenues (Tax_t) and expenses, public deficit reads:

$$Def_t = Debt_t^{cost} + Gbailout_t + G_t - Tax_t, \qquad (19)$$

where G_t are unemployment subsidies and $Debt_t^{cost}$ is the cost of sovereign debt. Deficits are financed on the bonds market, where banks buy the bonds issued by the government. Banks buy bonds with their net profits; if the total bank savings are lower than the stock of sovereign debt that needs to be refinanced, the central bank buys the residual part.

5.8 The Labour-Market Extension

A series of our contributions (Dosi et al., 2017, 2018a, 2018b, 2019, 2021) have extended the K+S model, accounting for decentralised interactions in the labour market between heterogenous workers and firms.

Such interactions occur within different institutions characterising wage-setting rules and labour markets, for example the presence (or not) of minimum wage, unemployment subsidy, firing rules, and so on.

The aggregate supply of labour L^S is still fixed, while the desired labour demand $L_{j,t}^d$ by any consumption-good firm j is determined by the ratio between the desired production $Q_{j,t}^d$ and the average productivity of its current capital stock $A_{j,t}$ (see Section 5.3):

$$L_{j,t}^d = \frac{Q_{j,t}^d}{A_{j,t}}. \tag{20}$$

A similar process is performed by firms i in the capital-good sector to define $L_{i,t}^d$, considering effective orders $Q_{i,t}$ and labour productivity in the current machine-producing technique $B_{i,t}$.[45] Given the existing labour force of the firm $L_{j,t-1}$, the desired variation of employment $\Delta L_{j,t}^d$ is then calculated as follows:

$$\Delta L_{j,t}^d = L_{j,t}^d - L_{j,t-1}. \tag{21}$$

Each firm j gets, in probability, a fraction of the applicant workers in its 'candidates queue', proportional to its market share $f_{j,t-1}$:

$$E(L_{j,t}^s) = \varpi L^S f_{j,t-1}, \tag{22}$$

where $\omega \in \mathbb{R}^+$ is a parameter defining the number of job 'queues' each seeker joins, in average, and $E(L_{j,t}^s)$ is the expected number of workers in the queue of firm j. As workers can apply to more than one firm at a time, firms may not be able to hire all workers in their queue, even when they mean to. Considering the set of workers in the candidates queue $\{\ell_{j,t}^s\}$, each firm has to select to whom to make a job (wage) offer. The set of desired workers $\{\ell_{j,t}^d\}$, among those in the queue $\{\ell_{j,t}^s\}$, is defined as:

$$\{\ell_{j,t}^d\} = \{\ell_{j,t} \in \{\ell_{j,t}^s\} : w_{\ell,t}^r < w_{j,t}^o \text{ and } \#\{\ell_{j,t}^d\} \leq \Delta L_{j,t}^d\}, \tag{23}$$

that is, the firm targets workers that would accept its wage offer $w_{j,t}^o$, considering the wage $w_{\ell,t}^r$ requested (if any), up to its demand of workers $\Delta L_{j,t}^d$. Therefore, the number of effectively hired workers (the size of set $\{\ell_{j,t}^h\}$) is:

$$\#\{\ell_{j,t}^h\} = \Delta L_{j,t} \leq \Delta L_{j,t}^d \leq L_{j,t}^s = \#\{\ell_{j,t}^s\}, \quad \Delta L_{j,t} = L_{j,t} - L_{j,t-1}. \tag{24}$$

---

[45] In what follows, we focus on the behaviour of consumption-good firms (indicated by the subscript j) in the labour market, as most workers are hired in this sector. However, capital-good firms operate under the same rules, including the hiring of R&D personnel, except they (i) follow the wage offers from top-paying firms in the consumption-good sector and (ii) present their job offers to workers before consumption-sector companies.

The model allows for *different institutional regimes in the labour market*. In the first one, which we call 'Fordist', there is an implicit pact among firms and workers, implying that the latter never voluntarily quit their jobs, while firms fire employees ($\Delta Q^d_{j,t} < 0$) only when experiencing negative profits $\Pi_{j,t-1}$ and shrinking production $\Delta Q^d_{j,t}$. Of course, firms exiting the market always fire all their workers. Conversely, only unemployed workers search for jobs.[46]

Wages are not bargained. Firm j unilaterally offers a wage $w^o_{j,t}$ based on past offers according to the following rule:

$$w^o_{j,t} = w^o_{j,t-1}[1 + \max(0, WP_{j,t})]. \tag{25}$$

The wage premium $WP_{j,t}$ is defined as:

$$WP_{j,t} = \psi_4 \frac{\Delta A_t}{A_{t-1}} + \psi_5 \frac{\Delta A_{j,t}}{A_{j,t-1}}, \quad \psi_2 + \psi_4 \leq 1, \tag{26}$$

with A_t being the aggregate labour productivity, $A_{j,t}$ the firm-specific productivity, and $\psi_4, \psi_5 \in [0,1]$ the parameters. The gains in labour productivity are then passed to workers via wage increases. Moreover, wages are linked not only to firm-specific performance but also to the aggregate productivity dynamics of the economy. Finally, note that $w^o_{j,t}$ is simultaneously applied to all existing workers of firm j, so there is no intra-firm differential in wages.[47]

Another archetype we study is the 'Competitive' regime, which can result from the introduction of structural reforms to spur flexibility in the labour market. In the new setting, wages adjust to labour market conditions: firms freely hire and fire in each period, and employees can actively search for better jobs all the time.

The wage $w^r_{\ell,t}$ requested by worker ℓ is a function of the individual unemployment condition and the past wage history. If the worker was unemployed in the previous period, the requested $w^r_{\ell,t}$ shrinks. More specifically, she will ask for the maximum between the unemployment benefit w^{un}_t (if available) and her own satisfying wage $w^s_{\ell,t}$:

$$w^r_{\ell,t} = \begin{cases} \max(w^{un}_t, w^s_{\ell,t}) & \text{if } \ell \text{ is unemployed in } t-1 \\ w_{\ell,t-1}(1+\epsilon) & \text{if } \ell \text{ is employed in } t-1 \end{cases}, \tag{27}$$

---

[46] In Dosi et al. (2018a, 2019) workers are also characterised by heterogenous skills that decay when they are unemployed, whereas they improve when they have a job.

[47] Wages are not unbounded, as each firm j can afford to pay a salary $w^o_{j,t}$ up to a maximum break-even wage $w^{max}_{j,t}$ that is the wage compatible with zero unit profits. This wage is defined as the product between (myopically) expected prices $p_{j,t-1}$ times existing productivity $A_{j,t-1}$:

$$w^o_{j,t} \leq w^{max}_{j,t}, \quad w^{max}_{j,t} = p_{j,t-1} A_{j,t-1}. \tag{28}$$

with the parameter $\epsilon \in \mathbb{R}^+$. The satisfying wage accounts for the recent wage history:

$$w^s_{\ell,t} = \frac{1}{T_s} \sum_{h=1}^{T_s} w_{\ell,t-h}, \qquad (29)$$

that is, as the moving average salary of the last $T_s \in \mathbb{N}^*$ periods.

Considering job applications and knowing the required number of workers $\Delta L^d_{j,t}$ to hire, the wage offered by each firm is the minimum that satisfies enough workers in its queue $\{\ell^s_{j,t}\}$. So, it is the highest wage requested by the cheapest available workers which fulfils $\Delta L^d_{j,t}$:

$$w^o_{j,t} = \max w^r_{\ell,t}, \quad \ell \in \{\ell^s_{j,t}\} \quad \text{and} \quad \#\{\ell^d_{j,t}\} \leq \Delta L^d_{j,t}. \qquad (30)$$

Employed workers search for better-paid jobs in each period. If a worker gets an offer from another firm n, she decides whether to quit or not from her current employer j if $w^o_{n \neq j,t} \geq w^r_{\ell,t}$. That is, worker ℓ quits firm j if she receives a wage offer $w^o_{n \neq j,t}$ from at least one firm n that is equal or higher than her required wage $w^r_{\ell,t}$.

Note that, differently from the original version of the K+S model, the market wage is not determined by exogenous institutional factors (see Equation 15), but it is microfounded via the local interactions of heterogeneous firms and workers. The unemployed benefit w^{un}_t is a fraction of the current average wage:

$$w^{un}_t = \varphi \bar{w}_{\ell,t-1}, \qquad (31)$$

where $\varphi \in [0,1]$ is a parameter and $\bar{w}_{\ell,t-1}$, the past period average wage. The government can also fix an institutional minimum wage w^{min}_t which imposes a lower bound to the firm-specific wage-setting behaviour:

$$w^{min}_t = w^{min}_{t-1}\left(1 + \psi_6 \frac{\Delta A_t}{A_{t-1}}\right). \qquad (32)$$

6 Empirical Validation

The Keynes+Schumpeter model does not allow for analytical, closed-form solutions. As discussed in detail in Section 4, this general ABM distinctive feature stems from the non-linearities present in agent decision rules and their interaction patterns, and it forces us to run computer simulations to analyse the properties of the stochastic processes governing the coevolution of micro and macro variables. In order to do so, the K+S model can be developed in the Laboratory for Simulation Development (LSD) platform (Valente, 2008), a free, open-source, user-friendly software framework dedicated to agent-based models. The online Appendix written by Marcelo C. Pereira (University of Campinas) provides all the steps to produce and analyse the results from the original Schumpeter meeting Keynes (K+S) model.[48] One can then perform extensive Monte Carlo simulation analyses to wash away across-simulation variability. As a consequence, the results presented in this section and the next one typically refer to across-run averages over one hundred replications and their standard-error bands.[49]

To begin with, we study whether the family of K+S models are able to reproduce *jointly* a wide range of macroeconomic and microeconomic stylised facts (**SF**, the 'benchmark' parametrisation is reported in Tables A.1 and A.2 Appendix A).[50] As mentioned earlier, if the K+S models successfully match empirical regularities concerning industrial dynamics as well as more structural relations between macroeconomic aggregates, this ought to be taken as a robust empirical validation (Fagiolo et al., 2017; Fagiolo & Roventini, 2017), lending plausibility to its use as a 'computational laboratory' to test different policy experiments. We report in Tables 1 and 2 the list of macro and micro empirical regularities that the K+S model is able to account for (which include those discussed by Haldane & Turrell, 2019). Note, to repeat, that the fact that a large number of very different micro and macro stylized facts are reproduced by the model makes our empirical validation exercises far more demanding than a simple polynomial-fitting exercise in the presence of some free parameters. At the same time, our macro agent-based model is able to account for a rich list of micro empirical regularities which cannot be structurally matched by any DSGE model given their representative-agent 'microfoundations'.

6.1 Macroeconomic Empirical Regularities

The macroeconomic empirical regularities matched by the K+S model are reported in Table 1. First, the generated time series show the emergence of endogenous self-sustained economic growth with persistent fluctuations (**SF1**, see Figure 3). Business cycles are punctuated by deep downturns (Stiglitz, 2014) and, in line with the empirical evidence (e.g. Fagiolo, Napoletano & Roventini 2008; Ascari, Fagiolo, & Roventini, 2015), the GDP growth-rate distribution exhibits fat tails (**SF2**, see Figure 4), revealing the coexistence of mild and deep downturns. Moreover, most recessions are short-lived; few last

---

[48] The online appendix can be found at this link: www.cambridge.org/EEVE_Roventini
[49] Simulation exercises suggest that, for the majority of statistics under study, Monte Carlo distributions are sufficiently symmetric and unimodal to justify the use of across-run averages as meaningful synthetic indicators.
[50] This section draws on Dosi, Fagiolo & Roventini (2010); Dosi et al. (2013; 2015; 2016a).

Table 1 Macroeconomic stylised facts replicated by the K+S model.

Stylised facts		Empirical studies (among others)
SF1	Endogenous self-sustained growth with persistent fluctuations	Burns and Mitchell (1946); Kuznets and Murphy (1966); Stock and Watson (1999); Zarnowitz (1985)
SF2	Fat-tailed GDP growth-rate distribution	Castaldi and Dosi (2009); Fagiolo, Napoletano, and Roventini (2008)
SF3	Recession duration exponentially distributed	Ausloos, Miskiewicz, and Sanglier (2004); Wright (2005)
SF4	Relative volatility of GDP, consumption and investment	Stock and Watson (1999)
SF5	Cross-correlations of macro variables	Napoletano, Roventini, and Sapio (2006); Stock and Watson (1999)
SF6	Pro-cyclical aggregate R&D investment	Walde and Woitek (2004)
SF7	Cross-correlations of credit-related variables	Leary (2009); Lown and Morgan (2006)
SF8	Cross-correlation between firm debt and loan losses	Foos, Norden, and Weber (2010); Mendoza and Terrones (2012)
SF9	Banking crises duration is right skewed	Reinhart and Rogoff (2009)
SF10	Fiscal costs of banking crises to GDP distribution is fat-tailed	Laeven and Valencia (2008)
SF11	Beveridge curve	
SF12	Okun curve	
SF13	Wage curve	
SF14	Matching function	
SF15	Endogenous volatility of productivity, unemployment, vacancy, separation, and hiring rates	Shimer (2005)

Table 2 Microeconomic stylised facts replicated by the K+S model.

Stylised facts		Empirical studies (among others)
SF16	Firm (log) size distribution is right-skewed	Dosi (2007)
SF17	Fat-tailed firm growth-rate distribution	Bottazzi and Secchi (2003, 2006)
SF18	Productivity heterogeneity across firms	Bartelsman and Doms (2000); Dosi (2007)
SF19	Persistent productivity differential across firms	Bartelsman and Doms (2000); Dosi (2007)
SF20	Lumpy investment rates at firm-level	Doms and Dunne (1998)
SF21	Firm bankruptcies are counter-cyclical	Jaimovich and Floetotto (2008)
SF22	Firm bad-debt distribution fits a power-law	Di Guilmi, Gallegati, and Ormerod (2004)
SF23	Fat-tailed unemployment time distribution	
SF24	Fat-tailed wage growth-rate distribution	
SF25	Heterogenous skill distribution	

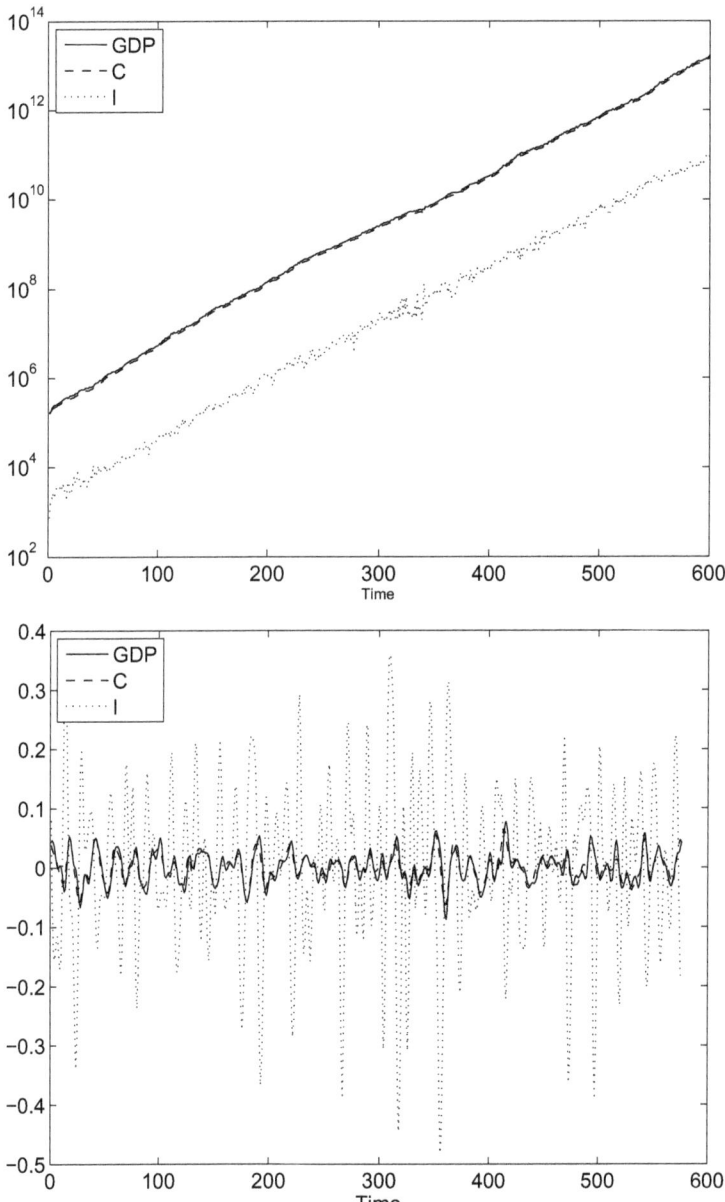

Figure 3 Output, consumption, and investment time series; *top:* logs; *bottom:* bandpass-filtered (6,32,12) series, reproduced from Dosi et al. (2015).

for long periods of time. The distribution of the duration of recessions generated by the model is exponential (**SF3**, see Figure 5), as found in empirical data (Ausloos, Miskiewicz, & Sanglier, 2004; Wright, 2005).

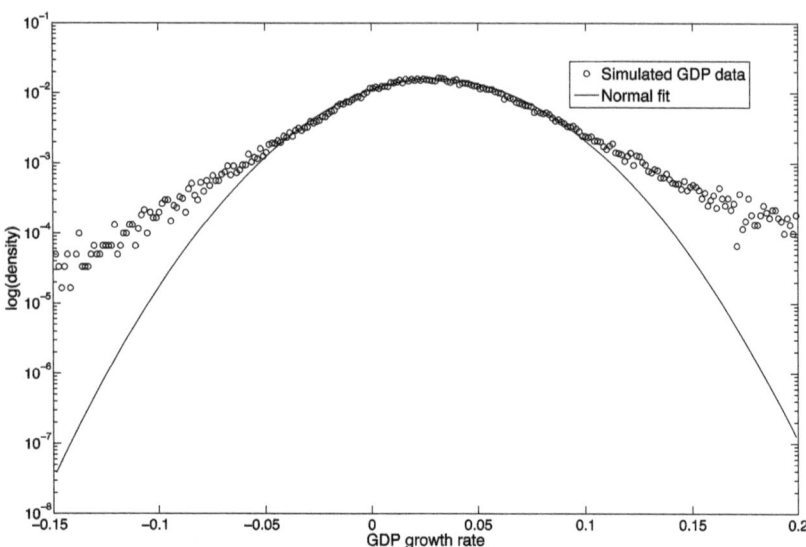

Figure 4 Distribution of real GDP growth rates: binned simulated densities (250 bins, 59,900 observations, circles) vs. normal fit (Dosi et al., 2015).

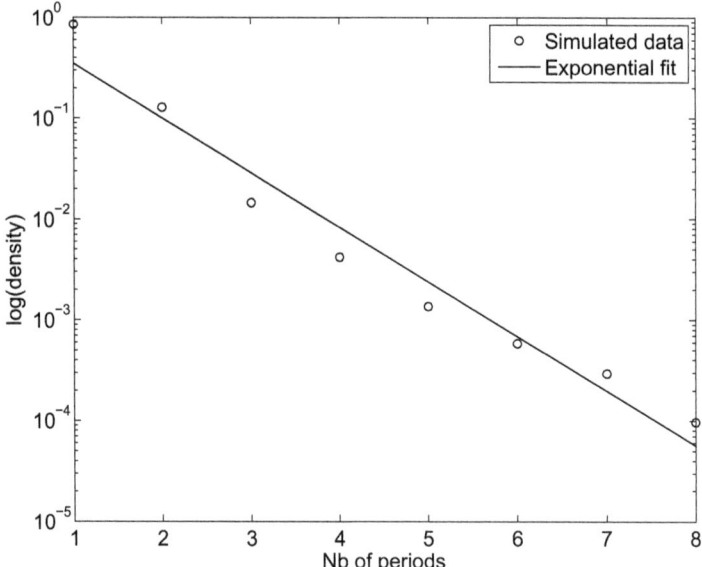

Figure 5 Exponential fit of recession durations (Dosi et al., 2015).

We then de-trend the macroeconomics series to study their behaviour at the business cycle frequencies. Well in tune with the empirical evidence (e.g. Stock & Watson, 1999; Napoletano, Roventini & Sapio, 2006), the fluctuations of aggregate consumption are smoother than those of GDP, whereas investment

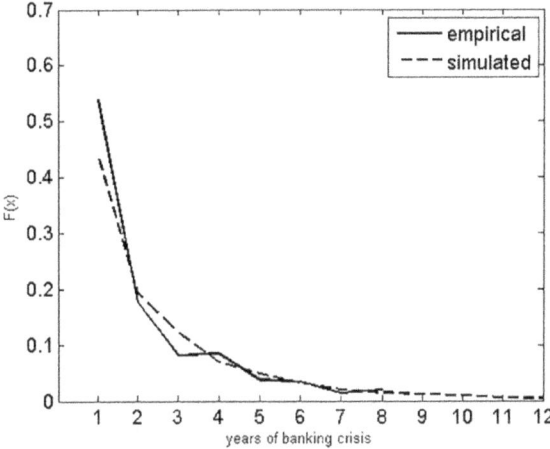

Figure 6 Distribution of banking crisis duration; simulated vs. empirical data. The length of a banking crisis is defined as the number of consecutive years with at least one banking failure in the country (Reinhart & Rogoff, 2009).

is more volatile than output (**SF4**, see Figure 3, bottom). Moreover, the co-movements between GDP and the most important macroeconomic variables are in line with what is found in real data (**SF5**, see Table 3): consumption is pro-cyclical and coincident; net investment, changes in inventories, productivity, nominal wages, and inflation are pro-cyclical; unemployment, prices, and mark-ups are counter-cyclical; the real wage is acyclical.[51] Finally, R&D investment is pro-cyclical (**SF6**; see e.g. Walde & Woitek, 2004).

The K+S models with heterogenous banks (Dosi et al., 2015) match additional stylized facts concerning *credit dynamics* and *banking crises*. To begin with, we find that bank profits as well as firms' total debt are pro-cyclical, while loan losses are counter-cyclical (**SF7**, see e.g. Lown & Morgan, 2006; Leary, 2009). Moreover, in line with the empirical evidence (Mendoza & Terrones, 2012), we find that credit surges anticipate banking crises: banks' loan losses are positively correlated with a lag with firm debt, suggesting that higher levels of credit precede bad debt, further depressing banks' equity (**SF8**, Foos, Norden, & Weber, 2010). Finally, the duration of banking crises, defined as a period in which at least one bank fails, has similar qualitative properties as the empirical one (**SF9**, see Figure 6, as well as Reinhart & Rogoff, 2009) and the distribution of the ratio of fiscal costs of banking crises to GDP is characterised by excess kurtosis and heavy tails (**SF10**).

---

[51] More details of the validation exercise can be found in Dosi, Fagiolo & Roventini (2006, 2008); Dosi, Fagiolo & Roventini (2010); Dosi et al. (2013, 2015).

Table 3 Correlation structure. Bpf: bandpass-filtered (6,32,12) series. Monte Carlo simulation standard errors in parentheses.

Series					Output (Bpf)				
(Bpf)	t−4	t−3	t−2	t−1	t	t+1	t+2	t+3	t+4
Output	−0.1022	0.1769	0.5478	0.8704	1	0.8704	0.5478	0.1769	−0.1022
	(0.0090)	(0.0080)	(0.0048)	(0.0014)	(0)	(0.0014)	(0.0048)	(0.0080)	(0.0090)
Consumption	−0.1206	0.0980	0.4256	0.7563	0.9527	0.9248	0.6848	0.3394	0.0250
	(0.0123)	(0.0129)	(0.0106)	(0.0062)	(0.0017)	(0.0018)	(0.0038)	(0.0058)	(0.0072)
Investment	−0.2638	−0.3123	−0.2646	−0.0864	0.1844	0.4473	0.5950	0.5757	0.4206
	(0.0102)	(0.0137)	(0.0182)	(0.0210)	(0.0206)	(0.0175)	(0.0139)	(0.0123)	(0.0129)
Net Investment	−0.0838	0.0392	0.2195	0.4010	0.5114	0.5037	0.3850	0.2105	0.0494
	(0.0122)	(0.0167)	(0.0216)	(0.0235)	(0.0211)	(0.0153)	(0.0103)	(0.0112)	(0.0138)
Ch. in Invent.	0.0072	0.1184	0.2349	0.2948	0.2573	0.1331	−0.0199	−0.1319	−0.1640
	(0.0081)	(0.0070)	(0.0060)	(0.0072)	(0.0090)	(0.0098)	(0.0097)	(0.0085)	(0.0067)
Employment	−0.3240	−0.1901	0.0796	0.4083	0.6692	0.7559	0.6451	0.4067	0.1555
	(0.0087)	(0.0123)	(0.0151)	(0.0160)	(0.0149)	(0.0120)	(0.0084)	(0.0069)	(0.0082)
Unempl. Rate	0.3357	0.2084	−0.0596	−0.3923	−0.6607	−0.7550	−0.6489	−0.4112	−0.1583
	(0.0083)	(0.0118)	(0.0147)	(0.0158)	(0.0148)	(0.0120)	(0.0084)	(0.0070)	(0.0082)
Productivity	0.1180	0.3084	0.5316	0.7108	0.7672	0.6656	0.4378	0.1664	−0.0609
	(0.0097)	(0.0088)	(0.0092)	(0.0093)	(0.0076)	(0.0067)	(0.0097)	(0.0126)	(0.0128)
Price	0.2558	0.3181	0.2702	0.0916	−0.1645	−0.3950	−0.5067	−0.4688	−0.3249
	(0.0167)	(0.0218)	(0.0235)	(0.0216)	(0.0198)	(0.0212)	(0.0225)	(0.0210)	(0.0176)
Inflation	−0.1070	0.0841	0.3110	0.4456	0.4021	0.1966	−0.0628	−0.2478	−0.2900
	(0.0151)	(0.0135)	(0.0175)	(0.0226)	(0.0228)	(0.0188)	(0.0154)	(0.0146)	(0.0131)
Mark-up	0.2183	0.1599	0.0411	−0.0988	−0.2040	−0.2361	−0.1968	−0.1226	−0.0580
	(0.0118)	(0.0088)	(0.0128)	(0.0184)	(0.0213)	(0.0206)	(0.0174)	(0.0135)	(0.0107)

Agent-Based Macroeconomics

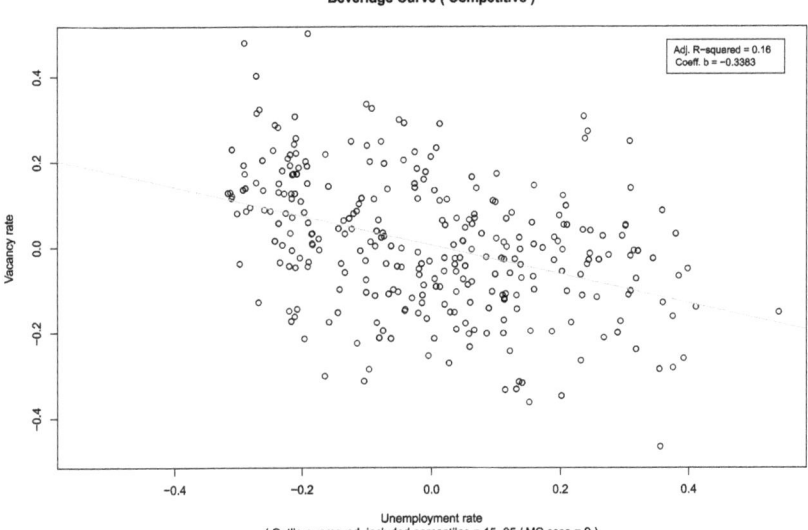

Figure 7 Beveridge curve (Dosi et al., 2017).

The micro foundation of the *labour market* structure and dynamics further enriches the list of empirical regularities matched by the model and also debunks the robustness of some other 'stylised facts'. More specifically, the extended K+S model is able to account for (roughly) the Beveridge curve (i.e. the negative correlation between unemployment and vacancy rates; see Figure 7 showing patterns as rough as the real ones), the Matching function (the positive correlation between vacancy-to-unemployment and job-finding rates; see Figure 8), the Wage curve, and the Okun curve (**SF11-14**; see Dosi et al., 2017, also for a detailed discussion of the other stylised facts). The model also replicates the analysis performed in Shimer (2005) concerning the correlation structure between unemployment, vacancy, job finding, separation, and productivity (**SF15**; see Table 4). On the debunking side, the results from our model add doubts on the robustness of the 'Phillips curves' (as already discussed by Solow, 1990; see also the recent Ratner & Sim, 2022), which might indeed be conditional on specific periods and institutional regimes.

6.2 Microeconomic Empirical Regularities

Beyond accounting for macroeconomic stylised facts, the family of the Schumpeter meeting Keynes models is also able to match the rather long list of microeconomic empirical regularities reported in Table 2.

Table 4 Correlation structure for Shimer (2005) statistics; u unemployment, v vacancy, f job finding, s separation, p productivity.

	u	v	v/u	f	s	p
Std. dev.	0.05	0.234	0.266	0.152	0.153	0.051
Autocorrelation	0.56	0.604	0.613	0.476	0.467	0.888
u	1.00	−0.612	−0.718	0.488	0.602	0.130
v		1.000	0.990	−0.532	−0.612	0.084
v/u			1.000	−0.555	−0.647	0.050
f				1.000	0.968	−0.068
s					1.000	−0.050
p						1.000

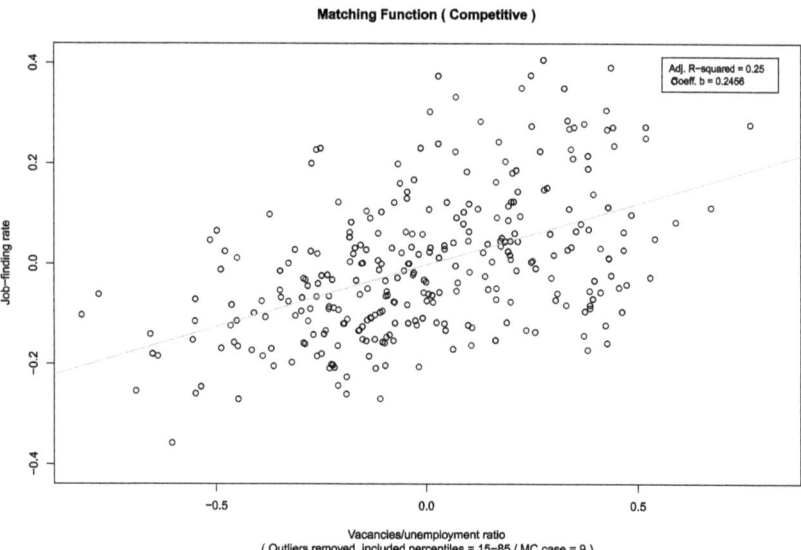

Figure 8 Matching function (Dosi et al., 2017).

Let us first consider those concerning the cross-sectional dynamics of firms (Bartelsman & Doms, 2000; Dosi, 2007). Rank-size plots and normality tests suggest that cross-section firm (log) size distributions are skewed and not lognormal (**SF16**; see Figures 9 and 10 and Table 5). Moreover, firm growth-rate distributions are 'tent-shaped' (**SF17**; see Table 6) with tails fatter than the Gaussian benchmark (Table 6; see Bottazzi & Secchi, 2003, 2006).

Turning to firm productivity, again in line with the empirical evidence (Bartelsman & Doms, 2000; Dosi, 2007), firms strikingly differ in terms

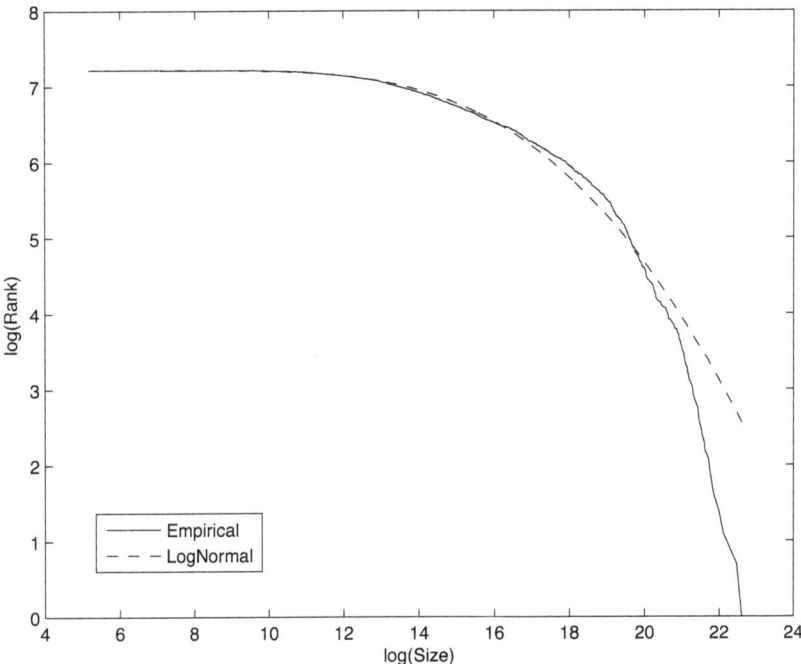

Figure 9 Pooled (year-standardised) capital-good firm sales distributions. Log rank vs. log size plots.

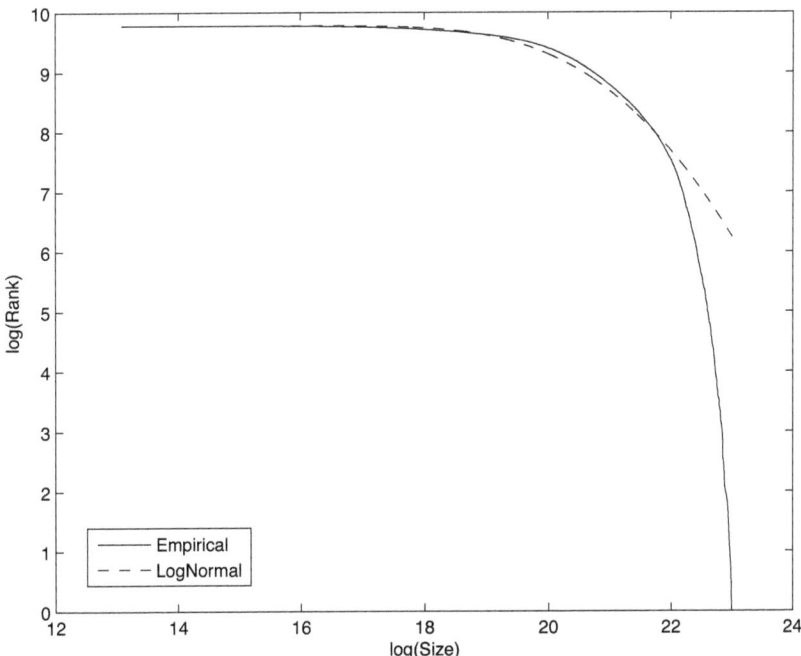

Figure 10 Pooled (year-standardised) consumption-good firm sales distributions. Log rank vs. log size plots.

Table 5 Log-size distributions, normality tests.

Industry	Jarque–Bera		Lilliefors		Anderson–Darling	
	stat.	p-value	stat.	p-value	stat.	p-value
Capital-good	20.7982	0	0.0464	0	4.4282	0
Consumption-good	3129.7817	0	0.0670	0	191.0805	0

Table 6 Growth-rate distributions, estimation of exponential-power parameters.

Series	b	Std. Dev.	a	Std. Dev.	m	Std. Dev.
Capital-good	0.5285	0.0024	0.4410	0.0189	−0.0089	0.0002
Consumption-good	0.4249	0.0051	0.0289	0.0037	0.0225	0.0001

of labour productivity (**SF18**; compare the standard deviations of labour productivity across firms plotted in Figure 11). Moreover, such productivity differentials persist over time (**SF19**; see the firm productivity autocorrelations reported in Table 7).[52]

The model is also able to generate as an emergent property investment lumpiness **SF20**; see Doms & Dunne, 1998; Caballero, 1999). Indeed, in each time step, consumption-good firms with 'near' zero investment coexist with firms experiencing investment spikes (see Figure 12 and relate it to Gourio & Kashyap, 2007).

New microeconomic stylised facts are matched when heterogenous banks and workers are added to the K+S model. Firms' bankruptcies are counter-cyclical (**SF21**, see Jaimovich & Floetotto, 2008), and the distribution of firms' bad debt at bankruptcy follows a power law (**SF22**), in tune with the empirical evidence (Di Guilmi et al., 2004). Finally, the labour-augmented K+S model replicates fat-tailed unemployment time distribution, fat-tailed wage growth rates distributions, and heterogenous worker-skill distributions (**SF23–25**).

---

[52] In the last 200 periods of the simulations, we consider the autocorrelation of firms that survived for at least 20 periods and we compute the industry average.

Table 7 Average autocorrelation of productivity. Standard deviations in parentheses.

Industry	t–1	t–2
Capital-good	0.5433	0.3700
	(0.1821)	(0.2140)
Consumption-good	0.5974	0.3465
	(0.2407)	(0.2535)

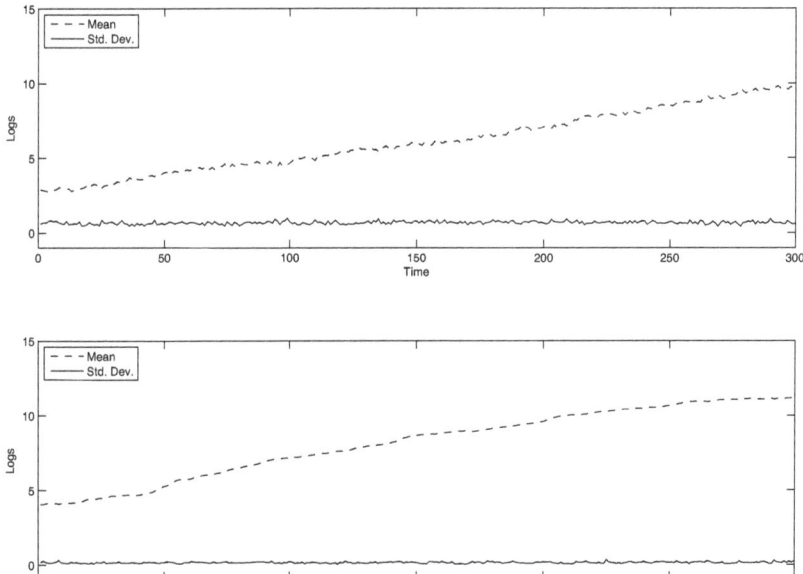

Figure 11 Firms' Productivity Moments (logs). First panel: capital-good firms. Second panel: consumption-good firms.

7 Policy Experiments

Given the extremely good interpretative performance of the Keynes meeting Schumpeter family of models, let us employ it to assess the short- and long-run impact of different policies.[53] In particular, we study the impact of changes in either the parameter values or the policy scenarios on the GDP and productivity growth rates, the ratio of public debt to GDP, output volatility, and the

---

[53] Interestingly, most statistical regularities concerning the structure of the economy appear to hold across an ample parameter range, under positive technological progress, even when policies undergo the changes we study in the rest of the Element.

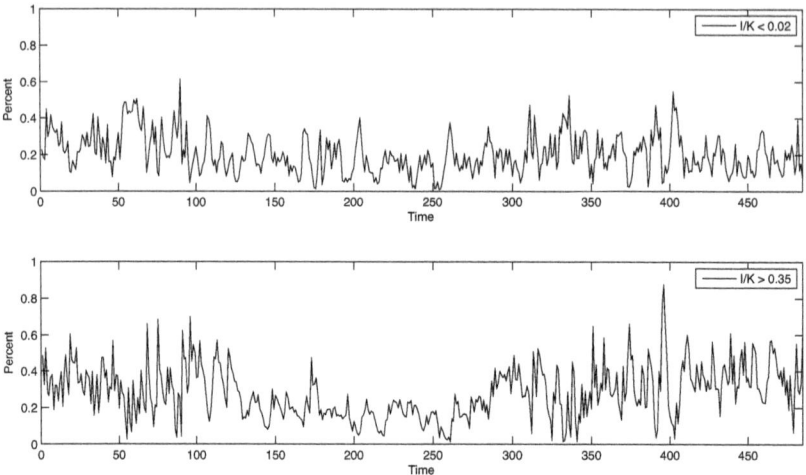

Figure 12 Investment lumpiness. First panel: share of firms with (near) zero investment; second panel: share of firms with investment spikes.

unemployment rate. We consider here policies affecting the two main sources of economic change, namely innovation (see Section 7.1) and demand (see Section 7.2), that is, the 'Schumpeterian' and 'Keynesian' engines of growth. Finally, we consider the relationship between income distribution and the effectiveness of policies (see Section 7.3). The full list of experiments is discussed in Dosi, Fagiolo & Roventini (2010); Dosi et al. (2013, 2015, 2017, 2018a, 2019, 2021). The corresponding parameter values are spelled out in Table A.3 in Appendix A.

7.1 Tuning the Schumpeterian Engine: Innovation Policy Matters

We start by considering how technology policies concerning firm search capabilities and technological opportunities affect the long-run performance of the economy and also its short-run dynamics (Section 7.1.1). Then we study a set of policies targeting appropriability conditions and the industrial dynamics of the economy (entry and competition; see Section 7.1.2).[54]

7.1.1 Technology Policies

Here we focus upon the 'Schumpeterian side' of the economy, holding the 'Keynesian engine' constant as compared with the benchmark scenario: Table 8 summarises the results. Let us start by turning off endogenous technological opportunities. In this case, the model collapses into a barebones 2-sector Solow

---

[54] The results of the experiments concerning technology and industry policies are drawn from Dosi, Fagiolo, & Roventini (2010).

Table 8 Technology policy experiments. Normalised values compared to the benchmark across experiments, for 100 simulation runs. Absolute value of the simulation t-statistic in parentheses; (**) significant at 5% level, (*) significant at 10% level.

Experiment	E1 Search capabilities		E2 Technological opportunities	
	low	high	low	high
GDP growth	0.917**	1.063**	0.774**	1.250**
	(7.425)	(5.657)	(25.491)	(22.274)
GDP volatility	1.020	0.958**	0.981	1.023*
	(1.505)	(3.198)	(1.411)	(1.919)
Unemployment rate	1.097	0.962	1.266**	0.956
	(1.345)	(0.592)	(4.031)	(0.658)

(1956) model in steady state, with fixed coefficients and zero growth (absent demographic changes).

In the first experiment, we change *firm search capabilities* (**E1**) approximated by the probabilities of accessing 'innovations' – no matter if failed or successful ones – (see the $\zeta_{1,2}$ parameters in Eqs. 4 and 5). We find that higher search capabilities positively influence the GDP rates of growth, while lowering the unemployment (see Table 8). Together, business cycle fluctuations are dampened possibly because a population of 'more competent' firms entails lower degrees of technological asymmetries across them and indeed also lower degrees of 'creative destruction', with more 'creative accumulation' of innovative capabilities.

What happens if one varies the *technological opportunities* of innovation and the ability to search for them? The second experiment (**E2**, see Table 8) explores such a case. As compared to the benchmark, we shift rightward and leftward the mass of the Beta distribution governing new technological draws (i.e. the parameters α_1 and β_1; see Section 5.2). Note that the support of the distribution remains unchanged, so that one could informally state that the *notional* possibilities of drift in the technological frontier remain unchanged, too. However, the pool of opportunities agents actually face gets either richer or more rarefied. As one could expect, we find that higher opportunities have a positive impact on the long-term rate of growth. Such policies also reduce the average unemployment, while slightly increasing GDP volatility (a mark of Schumpeterian 'gales of creative destruction'?).

7.1.2 Industrial Policies

The second set of experiments concerns the impact of policies affecting appropriability conditions and industry dynamics (experiments **E3**–**E6** in Table 9).

A tricky but relevant issue – both from the interpretative and normative points of view – regards the role of *appropriability conditions* (and, in particular, patents) as an incentive or an obstacle to innovation. The notion that some departure from the competitive zero profit condition is necessary in order to motivate capitalists to undertake search with their own money is at the core of the Schumpeterian (but also, earlier, Marxian) view of endogenous innovation. But how big should be such a departure? Neo-Schumpeterian models, as known, tend to assume monotonicity between degrees of appropriability and intensity of search, and, thus, rates of innovation (Aghion & Howitt, 1992). The assumption, other things equal, in turn rests upon some form of 'rational technological expectations'. Conversely, evolutionary models abhor the latter and assume much more routinized search behaviours. Recently, a large body of theoretical and empirical literature (see e.g. the contributions of Cimoli et al., 2014 and Dosi et al., 2022) have suggested that stricter property rights could be detrimental to innovation and growth. We exploit the modularity and flexibility of our agent-based model and introduce a patent system. More specifically, we test two alternative hypotheses (**E3**): in the 'length only' patent scenario, firms cannot imitate new technologies for a fixed number of periods; in the 'breadth' patent regime, firms are also forbidden to innovate around newly discovered technologies. We find that patents are detrimental both to long-run growth and to the short-run performance of the economy, being conducive to persistently higher unemployment rates (see Table 9). The negative impact of patents is stronger in the 'breadth' regime.[55]

We then test the effects of *firm entry* on competition and innovation by changing entrants' expected productivity (**E4**). We know empirically that most entrants are failures, but some are carriers of novel and potentially radical techniques and products (Dosi et al., 1997; Bellone et al., 2008; Aghion et al., 2009). This is sometimes dramatised in the evolutionary literature as a 'Schumpeterian Mark I' versus a 'Schumpeterian Mark II' scenario, meaning systematic innovative advantages for entrepreneurial entrants versus cumulative advantages of incumbents (see Dosi et al., 1995; Malerba & Orsenigo, 1995). How

---

[55] On purpose, we did not introduce any feedback between changes in IPR regimes and propensities to search. As discussed in Dosi, Marengo, and Pasquali (2006), such a link is absent in all historical evidence on the effects of changes in patenting regimes, on the one hand, and both investment in R&D and innovative intensity, on the other. However, in the agent-based model in Dosi et al. (2022), patents have a negative impact of the innovative performance of firms in the pharmaceutical industry even if such a feedback is taken into account.

Table 9 Industrial policy experiments. Normalised values compared to the benchmark across experiments, for 100 simulation runs. Absolute value of the simulation t-statistic in parentheses; (**) significant at 5% level, (*) significant at 10% level.

Experiment	E3 Patents		E4 Entrant expected prod.		E5 Market selection		E6 Antitrust	
	length	breadth	low	high	weak	strong	weak	strong
GDP growth	0.960**	0.647**	0.726**	1.492**	1.000	0.992	1.052**	1.083**
	(3.536)	(39.802)	(19.137)	(43.841)	(0.000)	(0.707)	(4.596)	(9.391)
GDP volatility	0.941**	0.780**	0.986	0.862**	1.038**	0.933**	0.863**	0.628**
	(4.515)	(17.981)	(0.792)	(12.148)	(2.916)	(5.857)	(12.040)	(94.626)
Unemployment rate	1.056	1.240**	1.308**	0.796**	1.169**	0.955	0.966	0.781**
	(0.768)	(3.074)	(3.376)	(3.191)	(2.364)	(0.659)	(0.546)	(3.814)

important are successful entrants? That is, from the normative point of view, what is the impact of policies favouring the entry of new competent firms? In our model, technological entry barriers (or advantages) are captured by the probability distribution over the 'technological draws' of entrants. Again, we hold constant the support over which the economy (i.e., every firm thereof) may draw innovative advances, conditional on the technology at any t. In this case we do it for sake of consistency: results, even more so, apply if different regimes also entail different probability supports. Let us first tune the Beta distribution parameters α_2 and β_2 (see Section 5.4). Our results are broadly in line with the evidence discussed in Aghion and Howitt (2007): *other things being equal*, the easiness of entry and competence of entrants bear a positive impact upon long-term growth, mitigate business cycle fluctuations, and reduce average unemployment (see Table 9). However, the ceteris paribus condition is equally important: the same aggregate growth patterns can be proved to be equally guaranteed by competent cumulative learning of incumbents (see the earlier exercises on search capabilities).

Finally, we explore the effect of *competition* (and relatedly, competition policies) by altering market selection in the consumption-good industry (**E5**) and by introducing antitrust policies in the capital-good sector (**E6**). An idea broadly shared across the economic discipline is that 'more competition is generally good'. In our model, that translates somewhat narrowly into a less imperfect access to information on prices by multiple heterogenous customers. In this case, in principle quite similar to the formally slimmer Phelps and Winter (1970), higher competition is reflected by the higher replicator dynamics parameter χ in Eq. 14. Simulation results suggest that a fiercer competition has negligible effects on growth, while it appears to somewhat reduce output volatility and average unemployment (see **E5** in Table 9). We then introduce antitrust policies by limiting the maximum market share of capital-goods firms to 75% (weak case) or 50% (strong case). The outcome of this policy experiment is a lower unemployment rate, smaller business cycle fluctuations and also higher GDP growth (see **E6** in Table 9; on this point see also Fogel, Morck, & Yeung, 2008). Note that such a property have little to do with any static 'welfare gains' – which our model does not explicitly contemplate – but rather with the multiplicity of producers, and thus of innovative search avenues, which antitrust policies safeguard.[56]

---

[56] The thrust of our results on policies affecting entry, competition, and variety preservation are indeed broadly in tune with the advocacy for 'evolutionary technology policies' in Metcalfe (1994b), while it runs against the so-called 'Schumpeterian hypothesis' according to which degrees of industrial concentration should be conducive to higher rates of innovation. The big caveat of the foregoing exercises, however, is that there are no increasing returns in innovative

7.2 Necessity of Keynesian Policies: Demand and Institutions Matter

So far, we have explored the effects of different 'Schumpeterian' policies and organisational set-ups over, for example, the rate of growth of the economy, the unemployment rates, and so on. The above sets of experiments clearly indicate that the sources of growth in the model lie in firms' ability to search efficiently and to develop improved products and processes, significantly affecting also the short-run dynamics of the economy. However, to repeat, such results are conditional on a 'Keynesian machine' well in place. What happens if we switch that off?

A first rough but very robust answer comes from the comparison between the foregoing regime with a set-up whereby all 'Keynesian' policies are turned off and the system lives under a 'pure Schumpeterian regime', holding, however, constant technological opportunities, search rules, and competition dynamics, as in the benchmark model (**E7**; see also Dosi, Fagiolo, & Roventini, 2010). Turning off the 'Keynesian' component implies a major jump to a different phase of the system, characterised by nearly zero growth and enormous fluctuations (see Table 10, column 2). This is because, by sustaining demand during

Table 10 Keynesian policy experiments. The 'strong' Schumpeterian regime is set with high technological opportunities and high search capabilities. Normalised values compared to the benchmark across experiments, for 100 simulation runs. Absolute value of the t-statistic in parentheses; (**) significant at 5% level, (*) significant at 10% level.

Experiment	E7 Schumpeterian regime		E8 Stabilisers		
	pure	strong	weak	strong	very strong
Subsidy rate	0	0	0.2	0.6	0.8
Tax rate	0	0	0.05	0.15	0.2
GDP growth	0.139**	0.437**	1.008	0.996	1.008
	(17.837)	(7.841)	(0.707)	(0.354)	(0.707)
GDP volatility	19.611**	19.173**	1.902**	0.779**	0.722**
	(47.186)	(34.426)	(28.119)	(20.808)	(24.405)
Unemployment rate	10.962**	7.327**	2.413**	0.789**	0.562**
	(37.639)	(24.353)	(8.846)	(3.738)	(8.271)

---

research. If there were, then size would affect the latter. And this would offer support to some form of 'Schumpeterian hypothesis'.

recessions, countercyclical Keynesian policies also smooth investment over the business cycle. Low demand indeed reduces both consumption-goods firms' investment and capital-goods firms' R&D expenses, thus rates of innovation and productivity growth. Such a vicious circle of low R&D, low economic growth, and high volatility is in line with previous accounts by Stiglitz (1994) and Aghion et al. (2008) and Aghion et al. (2010), in particular in the presence of credit market imperfections (Aghion, Hemous, & Kharroubi, 2014).

The experiments discussed earlier indicate that Schumpeterian and Keynesian policies affect, together, short-term economic indicators (e.g., output volatility and employment), as well as long-term ones (e.g., GDP growth). Still, these experiments were implemented considering 'everything else being equal': an active technology policy was tested, taking as fixed the fiscal side of the model, and the other way round. Could technology policies be a substitute for a lack of fiscal policies? We test this proposition by experimenting with a 'strong Schumpeterian regime' (high search capabilities and technological opportunities) combined with a zero fiscal policy scenario (no taxes and unemployment subsidies). Table 10 (column 3) shows that in this case average GDP growth falls by 56% with respect to the baseline. Notice that it is exactly the net effect from both policies. Indeed, the former increases the average GDP growth rate (respectively, by 6% and 25%), while the latter has a negative impact amounting to a 86% cut in the long-run rate of output growth. It follows that Keynesian policies are *complementary* to Schumpeterian ones, as the latter alone cannot sustain a stable growth path.

In the K+S benchmark model, taxes and unemployment subsidies act as automatic stabilisers, dampening business cycle fluctuations. In experiment **E8** (Dosi et al., 2010), we jointly modify the intensity of these stabilisers by altering the tax and subsidy rates tr and φ (see Section 5.6). Results in Table 10 show the impact of Keynesian fiscal policies upon *long-run* economic growth and *short-run* dynamics. In the presence of the 'good phase' of the system (to repeat, *with positive tax and subsidy*; see Figure 13), higher levels of automatic stabilisers do not affect average GDP, but they further stabilise output fluctuations: GDP volatility and unemployment rates fall as taxes and subsidy rates are jointly increased.[57]

---

[57] The foregoing results are robust to alternative institutional regimes governing the labour market captured by the parameters affecting the wage rate (see Eq. 15). In particular, we may allow wages to move as a (negative) function of the unemployment rate and to respond to inflation. This supports both our previous results about the importance of the 'Keynesian engine' as a necessary ingredient of sustained long-run growth and Keynes's own insights (Keynes, 1936) about the irrelevance, at best, of wage cuts in reducing unemployment: see Dosi, Fagiolo, & Roventini (2010), Dosi et al. (2017, 2021) and Section 7.2.2 where we perform different policy experiments with the extended version of the K+S model which explicitly take into account the

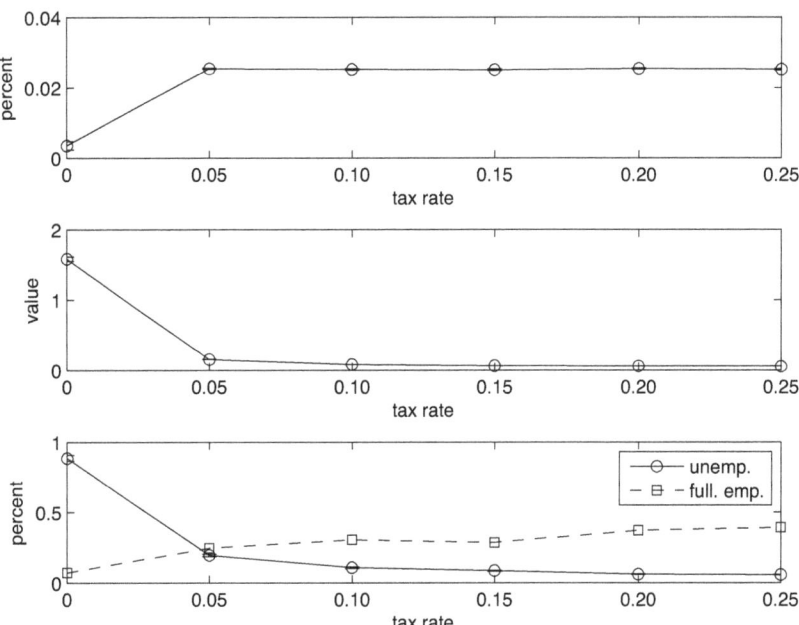

Figure 13 Fiscal policy experiments (Dosi, Fagiolo, & Roventini, 2010). First panel: average output growth rate. Second panel: bandpass-filtered output standard deviation. Third panel: average unemployment rate (unemp.) and full-employment frequency (full emp.). In such policy experiments, the unemployment subsidy rate (φ) is four times the tax rate.

7.2.1 Fiscal Austerity Rules

Let us now further test the impact of Keynesian fiscal policies by studying the impact of different *austerity fiscal rules* akin to those implemented in the European Union. We first consider a fiscal rule mimicking the European Stability and Growth Pact (SGP; see Dosi et al., 2015) which constrains the public deficit to 3% of GDP, forcing the government to cut unemployment subsidies until the deficit-to-GDP target is reached. We then introduce the stricter Fiscal Compact (FC) rule, where the the SGP deficit limit is supplemented by a debt-reduction rule: if the ratio of public debt to GDP is over the SGP target of 60%, it should be reduced by 1/20th (5%) of the difference between the current and target levels in every year.[58] In both regimes, unemployment benefits are

---

impact on wages and employment of the local interactions of heterogenous firms and workers in the labour market.

[58] It is not the exact replica of the Fiscal Compact as we do not consider the limit to the structural deficit. Still, we are close in spirit to the FC as we jointly consider the debt reduction and the 3%-deficit rules, and we also consider the escape clause in case of recession.

Table 11 Fiscal policy experiments. Normalised values compared to the benchmark across experiments, for 100 simulation runs. Absolute value of the *t*-statistic in parentheses; (**) significant at 5% level, (*) significant at 10% level.

Experiment	E9				
	SGP	*SGP$_{ec}$*	*FC*	*FC$_{ec}$*	*FC$_{ec}^{spread}$*
GDP growth	0.527**	0.995**	0.572**	0.992**	0.997**
	(6.894)	(0.876)	(6.499)	(1.388)	(0.524)
GDP volatility	14.645**	1.408**	16.204**	1.624**	1.530**
	(7.466)	(5.856)	(7.848)	(7.166)	(6.962)
Unemployment rate	5.692**	5.706**	1.419	1.948**	1.679**
	(8.095)	(2.088)	(7.585)	(3.928)	(3.139)
Public Debt/GDP	+∞	1.763**	+∞	4.078**	2.590**
		(0.774)		(2.472)	(1.483)

eventually cut to comply with the fiscal rules. In line with the European Union fiscal framework, we introduce escape clauses (*SGP$_{ec}$* and *FC$_{ec}$*) which freeze austerity rules in case of negative GDP growth. Finally, we account for the possible existence of a positive feedback mechanism going from the level of public debt to its financing cost by adding a risk premium to the interest rate on sovereign bonds. In such a scenario with the FC fiscal rule (*FG$_{ec}^{spread}$*), 'frugal' governments should pay a lower interest rate on their stock of public debt.

The results from the fiscal rule experiments (**E9**; see Table 11) point, again, to the necessity of active fiscal policy to stabilise the economy and achieve steady growth. Indeed, we find that in the 'harsh' case, when the *SGP* fiscal rule is applied, average GDP growth is halved compared to the baseline scenario, and GDP volatility and unemployment are respectively 14 and 5 times higher. Moreover, the public-debt-to-GDP ratio explodes due to the joint expansion of debt and the shrinkage of output, showing the *self-defeating* effect of fiscal discipline policies. The negative impact of austerity fiscal rules is even more harmful in the Fiscal Compact scenario. When escape clauses are present (*SGP$_{ec}$* e *FC$_{ec}$*), the long-run harmful effects of fiscal discipline disappear, but volatility and unemployment rates are still significantly higher with respect to the case where fiscal policy is unconstrained (see Table 10). These findings shed light on the non-linear effects of fiscal policies on GDP growth (see Figure 13), as the halt to fiscal support during recessions is likely to transform them in depressions. Finally, the results are also robust when the spread on sovereign bonds is linked to the ratio between public debt and GDP (*FG$_{ec}^{spread}$*): austerity

Table 12 Fiscal rule – microeconomic indicators. Normalised values compared to the benchmark across experiments, for 100 simulation runs. Absolute value of the *t*-statistic in parentheses; (**) significant at 5% level, (*) significant at 10% level.

Experiment	E9 Fiscal rule SGP	
Innovation creation in the capital-good sector		
Share of successful innovators	0.946**	(2.762)
Productivity growth	0.980**	(2.269)
Productivity dispersion	0.917**	(6.538)
Innovation diffusion in the consumption-goods sector		
Productivity growth	0.889**	(3.912)
Productivity dispersion	0.865**	(3.429)
Investment rate	0.973	(1.275)
Duration of best vintage	1.037**	(3.927)
Productivity growth best vintage	0.954**	(34.446)
Relative distance between best and worst vintages	0.970**	(2.432)

rules worsen both short- and long-run economic dynamics without improving public finances.[59]

One of the advantages of employing agent-based models to study economic problems is the possibility of zooming upon the microeconomic level to better understand the emergent properties observed at the macro level. The wealth of microeconomic data generated by the simulations can indeed be employed to build new statistics which can shed light on macroeconomic dynamics. This is what we do with the microeconomic indicators displayed in Table 12, which allow us to study the underlying micro-level mechanisms at the origin of the aggregate outcomes observed when fiscal rules are in place (see Dosi et al., 2016). First, we consider the consumption-good sector. We find that firms' investment rate falls due to the lower consumption demand. This slows down the diffusion of the new vintages of machines with state-of-the-art technology thus depressing productivity growth. The negative impact of austerity policies percolates to the capital-good sector. There, the lower sales experienced by capital-good firms reduce their R&D investment. As a result, innovation

---

[59] Such a conclusion holds also when the bond-spread channel is considered with the SGP fiscal rule. The results are reported in Dosi, Fagiolo, & Roventini (2010).

falls, slowing down the productivity growth of the industry (see Table 12). The reduced creation and diffusion of innovations imply that the best vintage stays undisputed for a longer period, and the productivity frontier grows at a slower pace. Indeed, this represents a power evidence of the (virtuous or perverse) feedback between the 'Keynesian' demand-generating mechanism and the long-term movement of the technological frontier.

7.2.2 Labour Market Reforms

In contrast to DSGE models, macroeconomic agent-based models can easily test different combinations of policies concerning the labour and credit markets. We undertake two sets of policy experiments. In the first one, we study the interactions between fiscal policies and different labour-market institutions governing wage formation, firm firing rules, etc. (**E10**). In the next section, we will present the second policy combination scenario, where we interact fiscal policies with monetary policy rules (**E11**).

How do labour market institutions affect the short- and long-run performance of the economy and interact with fiscal policy rules? In the 'Fordist' regime, the labour-augmented K+S model presented in Section 5.8 depicts a scenario where (i) wages are insensitive to the labour-market conditions and indexed to aggregate and firm-specific gains; (ii) there is a sort of covenant between firms and workers concerning 'long-term' employment, as firms fire only when their profits get negative, while employed workers do not seek for alternative occupations; (iii) labour market institutions contemplate a minimum wage fully indexed to aggregated economy productivity and unemployment benefits financed by taxes on profits. The 'Fordist' regime captures the main features of the Trente Glorieuses (roughly the three decades after World War II) characterised by low probability of workers being fired, wage dynamics mostly rigid to the business cycle, wage growth rate indexed upon productivity growth, a shrinking degree of inequality, and significant, tax-based unemployment benefits.

At the opposite end when the labour market is characterised by the 'Competitive' regime, (i) flexible wages respond to unemployment and market conditions; (ii) firms have a stronger bargaining power with regard to wages and employment, which they seamlessly adjust according to the planned production level; (iii) employed workers search for better paid jobs; (iv) the minimum wage and unemployment benefit institutions are weaker or even absent. The Competitive scenario is akin to the labour market presented in introductory-level Neoclassical economics textbooks and it captures the structural reforms suggested by the Washington Consensus and the European Union (Fitoussi & Saraceno, 2013).

Table 13 Labour-market reform experiments. Normalised values compared to the benchmark across experiments, for 50 simulation runs. P-values in parentheses; (**) significant at 5% level, (*) significant at 10% level.

Experiment		E10	
	Fordist (baseline)	Competitive (ratio)	Competitive & Fiscal Compact (ratio)
GDP growth	0.02	0.78**	0.68**
		(0.01)	(0.00)
GDP volatility	0.11	0.86**	1.19**
		(0.01)	(0.00)
Unemployment rate	0.02	8.93**	10.96**
		(0.00)	(0.00)
Profit share	0.22	1.02**	1.03**
		(0.00)	(0.00)
Income concentration	0.05	3.60**	5.09**
		(0.00)	(0.00)

We simulate the model in the Fordist and Competitive regimes (see Table 13). Simulation results show that labour market flexibility *worsens* the performance of the economy both over short- and long-run horizons. Indeed, the unemployment rate is higher in the Competitive regime, while the Fordist regime entails stronger productivity and output growth. Note that the *degradation* of economic performance increases with the degree of labour-market flexibility: in Dosi et al. (2017) we find that in the Competitive scenario nearest to 'market perfection' (absence of minimum wage, unemployment benefits, and employment protection rules), the modelled economic system is most of the time near to collapse with basically zero long-term economic growth and extremely high unemployment rates and volatility. This result is in line with those obtained earlier when the Keynesian machine is switched off. Moreover, we find that *hysteresis* is much more likely to emerge in the Competitive regime, thus worsening macroeconomic dynamics at all frequencies (see Figure 14 and the results in Dosi et al., 2018a).

The negative impact of the Fiscal Compact rule is magnified when the labour market is characterised by a higher level of flexibility (see Table 13).[60] Indeed, the policy combination of austerity rule and competitive labour-market reforms

---

[60] Note that the results in Table 13 and Dosi et al. (2019) are obtained in the presence of active labour-market policies directed at promoting job search and providing training to unemployed workers. The results would just be worse in absence of such policies.

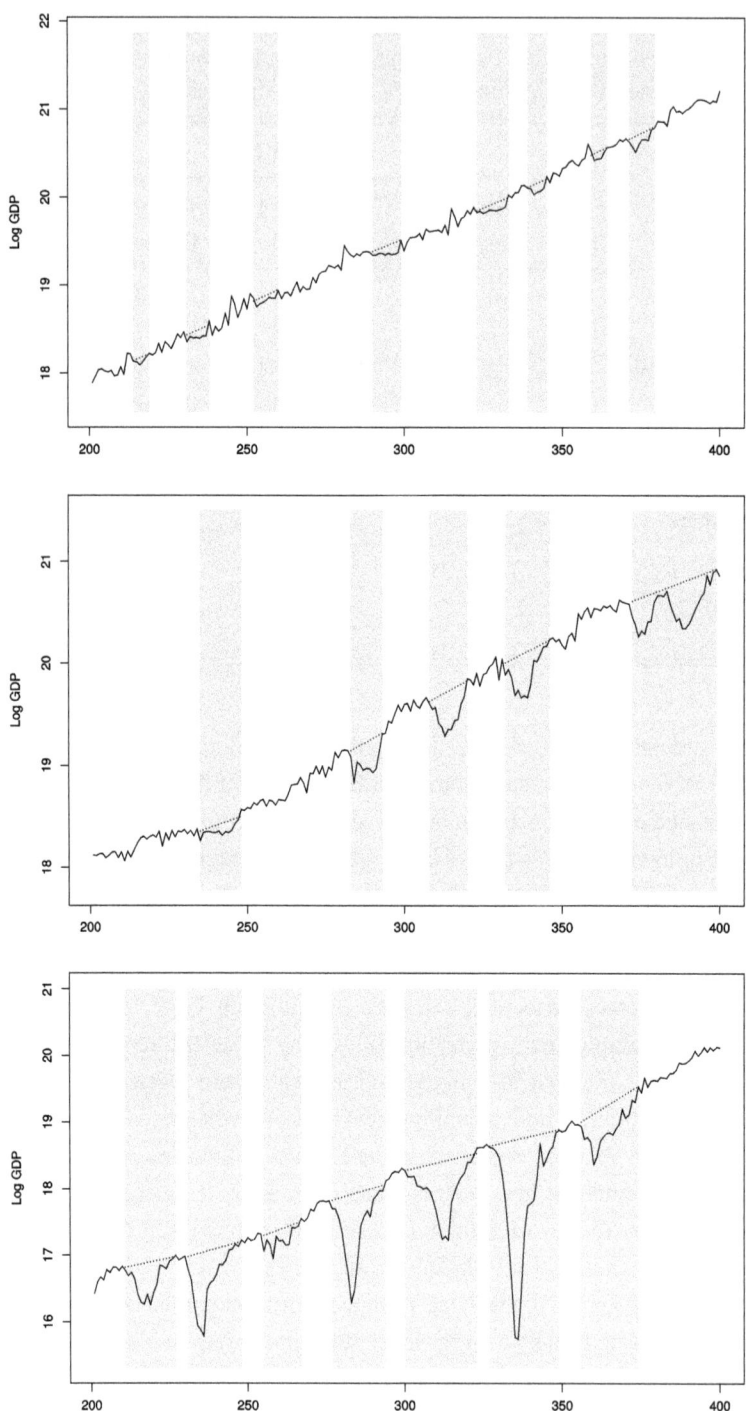

Figure 14 GDP long-term trend recovery after crisis (Dosi et al., 2019). Typical simulation run. Top: Fordist; middle: Competitive; bottom: Competitive and Fiscal Compact rule. Dashed line: pre-crisis trend | grey boxes: trend recovery period.

permanently damage the GDP growth trajectory and spur unemployment, leading to the emergence of *super-hysteresis* (see Figure 14; Dosi et al., 2018a and Cerra et al., 2023). Also in this case austerity policies are self-defeating, leading to higher levels of public debt (see the detailed analysis in Dosi et al., 2019). To sum up, our results clearly show that the policy combination grounded on 'structural reforms' to increase labour flexibility and austerity fiscal policies (the so called Berlin–Washington consensus; see Fitoussi & Saraceno, 2013) have a deeply negative impact on the short- and long-run performance of the economy, and also on public finances.

7.2.3 Monetary Policy

In the foregoing experiments, the central bank followed a 'conservative' monetary policy as it applied a standard Taylor rule which adjusts the baseline interest rate only to the inflation gap (TR_π; see Eq. 18). In line with the recent monetary policy strategy of the Federal Reserve (Yellen, 2014), we now let the central bank follow a dual-mandate monetary policy ($TR_{\pi,U}$) by including an adjustment to the unemployment gap ($\gamma_U > 1$), with a 5% unemployment rate target (**E11**).

Simulation results reported in Table 14 show that when fiscal policy is unconstrained and the central bank commits to both price and employment stabilisation, monetary policy positively affects the performance of the economy. When the SGP fiscal rule is activated, the positive impact of the dual-mandate monetary policy is reinforced, as it contributes to alleviate the pains caused by fiscal-consolidation policies and to stabilise public finance. The dual-mandate Taylor rule dominates the conservative one also in the presence of the FC rule, when fiscal clauses are activated and when the bond-spread channel is taken into account.[61]

The better performance of the $TR_{\pi,U}$ rule over the TR_π depends on the presence of bank credit transmission channels of monetary policy (see e.g. Bernanke, Gertler, & Gilchrist, 1999 and Boivin, Kiley, & Mishkin, 2010) due to the interaction of the dual-mandate monetary policy with the Basel rule governing changes in credit supply (see Eq. 17). By reducing the pro-cyclicality of the Basel macroprudential rule, the dual mandate therefore compensates its destabilising effect and provides both banks and firms with a stronger financial record at the eve of an economic crisis. Indeed, with a dual-mandate monetary policy rule, the interest rate goes up during expansions as a response to low unemployment levels. This boosts banks' profit margin and net worth,

---

[61] The results are reported in Dosi et al. (2015). Note also that for every type of fiscal policy, the dual-mandate Taylor rule (slightly) increases the inflation rate, but in any case the average inflation rate is quite small.

Table 14 Monetary policy experiments. Normalised values compared to the benchmark across experiments, for 100 simulation runs. Absolute value of the t-statistic in parentheses; (**) significant at 5% level, (*) significant at 10% level.

Experiment	E11		
	$norule, TR_{\pi,U}$	SGP, TR_{π}	$SGP, TR_{\pi,U}$
GDP growth	1.019**	0.527**	1.014
	(3.730)	(6.894)	(1.157)
GDP volatility	0.865**	14.645**	2.760**
	(6.018)	(7.466)	(2.401)
Unemployment rate	0.322**	5.692**	0.909
	(5.903)	(8.095)	(0.555)
Public Debt/GDP	−50.648**	+∞	−45.545**
	(30.377)		(9.011)

while cooling down firms' borrowing. When the downturn arrives, the interest rate goes down and loan losses increase. However, banks' capital buffers allow them to better resist the negative shocks and provide more credit vis-à-vis the conservative Taylor rule scenario.

7.3 Income Inequality and Policy Effectiveness: Distribution Matters

In macro agent-based models, policy experiments can be performed in alternative scenarios concerning the structural and institutional characteristics of the economy, as well as with respect to personal and functional income distributions. Admittedly, all the incumbent K+S models are constrained by the assumption of initial levels of mark-ups of the firm which partly 'anchor' the *average functional income* distribution thereafter. This indeed is a drawback to be overcome in the near future. Still, even under this limitation, it is highly informative to study the impact of alternative combination of policies on the level of functional income inequality in the economy (**E12**), and, even more so, on the personal distribution with respect to wage earners.

The policy experiments performed so far have been carried out for a given level of income inequality. Indeed, the firm-specific mark-ups of consumption-good firms fluctuate around the initial peg; see Eqs. 11 and 12. By tuning up and down the level of the *initial* mark-up rate, we can (admittedly, still in a rudimentary way) change the long-term functional income distribution.

This allows us to study how inequality affects the dynamics of the economy, as well as the results produced by the different mixes of policies spotlighted in the previous section. In Dosi et al. (2013), we found that a higher level of inequality in the wage/profit distribution increases the effects of fiscal policies. This is in line with many works suggesting that increasing levels of inequality have contributed to depress aggregate demand and to weigh down private indebtedness, thus setting the stage for the Great Recession (Fitoussi & Saraceno, 2010; Stiglitz, 2012; Kumhof & Rancière, 2015).

Given such premises, let us study how our target variables evolve when we modify the income distribution under the benchmark scenario where fiscal rules are not activated and the central bank follows a conservative Taylor rule. First, rising firm margins, reflected, of course, by higher income inequality, impact aggregate demand, and they thus affect macroeconomic dynamics (see Figure 15). If, on the one hand, the average GDP growth rate is stable for different levels of mark-up, on the other hand, the (slightly) U-shape pattern displayed by GDP volatility, unemployment rates, likelihood of economic crisis and public-debt-to-GDP ratio reveal the existence of two 'regimes'. When mark-ups are low, firms have a reduced ability to finance their investment with their own accumulated profits and rely more on credit, increasing the size of banks and the cost of banking crises. Therefore the size of the banking sector is negatively associated with the mark-up rate. If mark-ups are too low, firms' higher failure rates weaken the banking sector, thus curbing the supply of credit. As a consequence, a higher proportion of financially constrained firms reduces production and investment, leading to higher unemployment rates. When income distribution is too skewed towards profits, firms do not invest because demand is too low. This spurs GDP volatility, unemployment, and public debt (Dosi et al., 2013 and 2015).

Let us now consider the impact of fiscal rules across different functional inequality scenarios. Income distribution and fiscal policies can interact via two channels. First, tighter limits on budget deficits can further depress aggregate demand, thus worsening firms' financial constraints and increasing the likelihood of banking crises which require public bailout. Second, when the income distribution is more biased towards profits, fiscal policy is more needed to sustain an (otherwise low) consumption demand (see Dosi et al., 2015). Simulation results show that for every level of functional income inequality, the SGP and FC fiscal rules increase the instability of the economy (see Figure 16) and inflate the ratio between public debt and GDP. Moreover, fiscal discipline appears to be *more harmful* as the income distribution becomes more biased towards profits. Indeed, even if in this regime firms have access to both internal and external financial resources, they do not invest for a lack of aggregate demand,

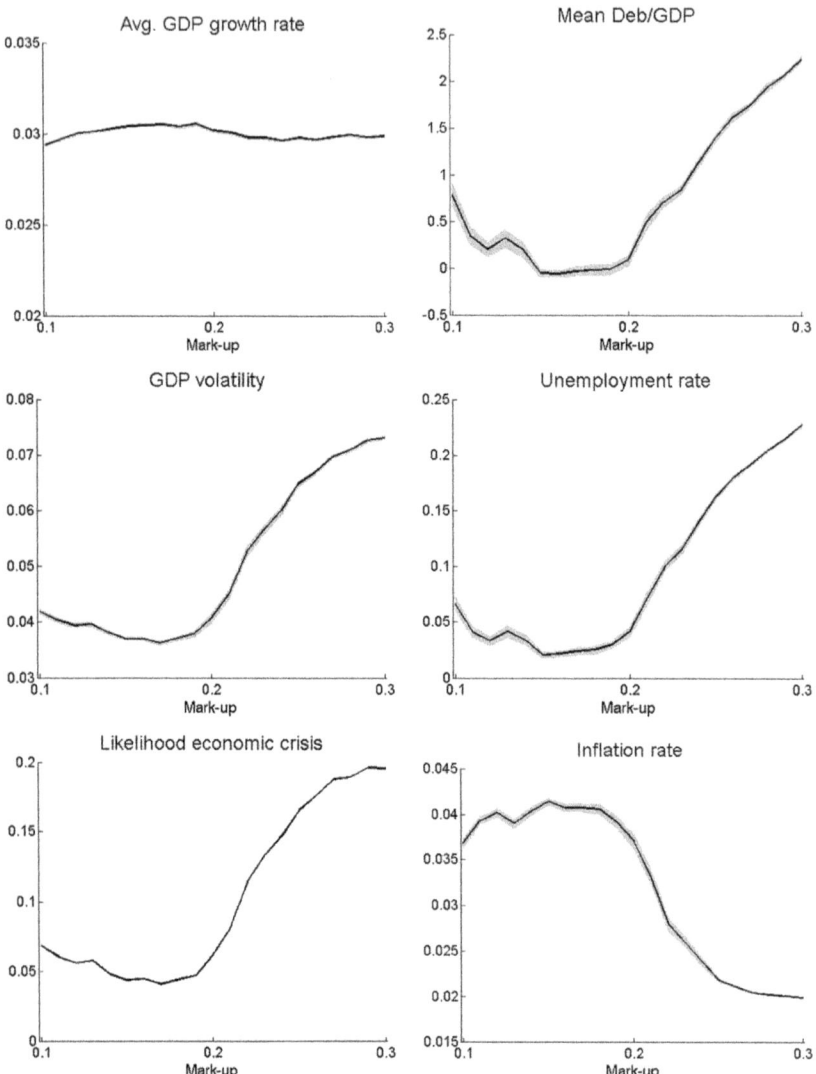

Figure 15 Income distribution and macroeconomic dynamics (Dosi et al., 2015). Confidence-interval bands are shown in a lighter colour and are computed as plus or minus two Monte Carlo standard errors.

which in turn reduces the average GDP growth rate and leads to the explosion of the public-debt-to-GDP ratio.[62] Further exercises suggest that when the escape clauses are in place, they prevent the activation of fiscal rules up to 40% of the periods (Figure 16, bottom right), thus reducing their negative impact on the

---

[62] In Figure 16 we report the share of simulations that end in a debt crisis, identified as an average public debt-to-GDP ratio above five.

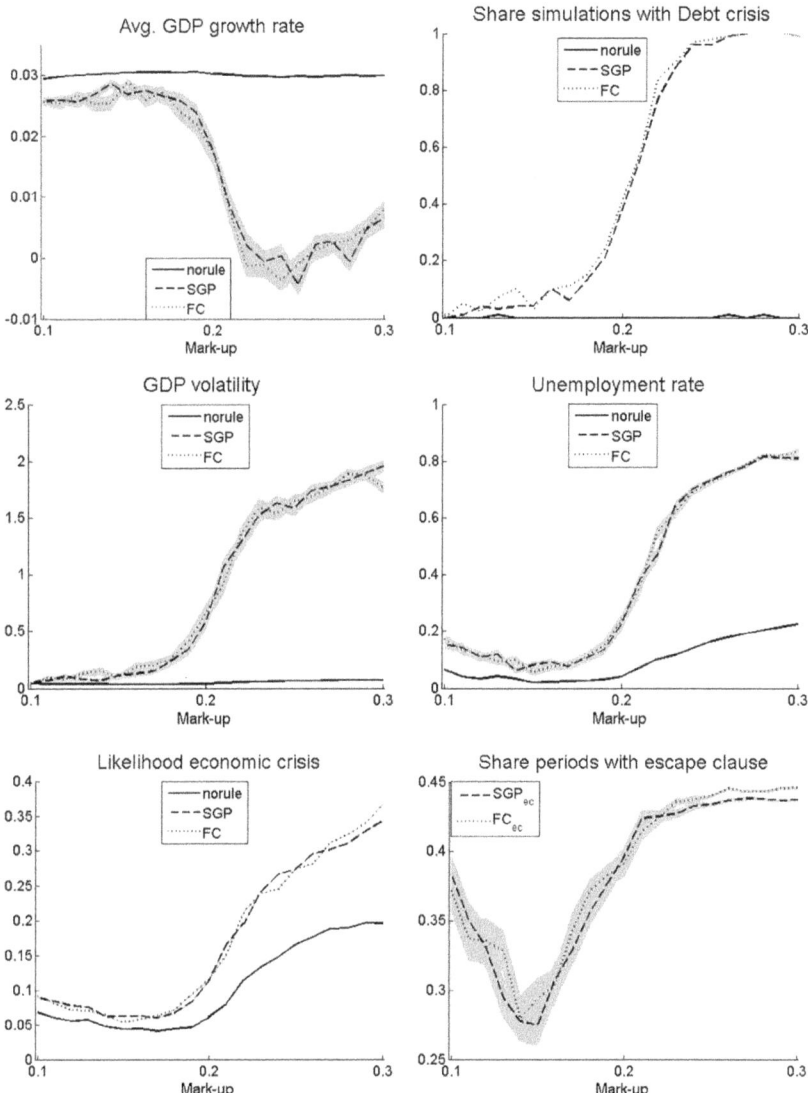

Figure 16 Fiscal rule experiments (Dosi et al., 2015). Confidence-interval bands are shown in a lighter colour and are computed as plus or minus two Monte Carlo standard errors.

dynamics of the economy. Nonetheless, in line with our previous results, the economy keeps on being more unstable and we keep observing a perverse effect of fiscal rules on public debt. Such results are also confirmed in the sovereign bond-spread adjustment scenario.

How does monetary policy interact with income inequality? In the presence of unconstrained fiscal policies, the dual-mandate Taylor rule outperforms the

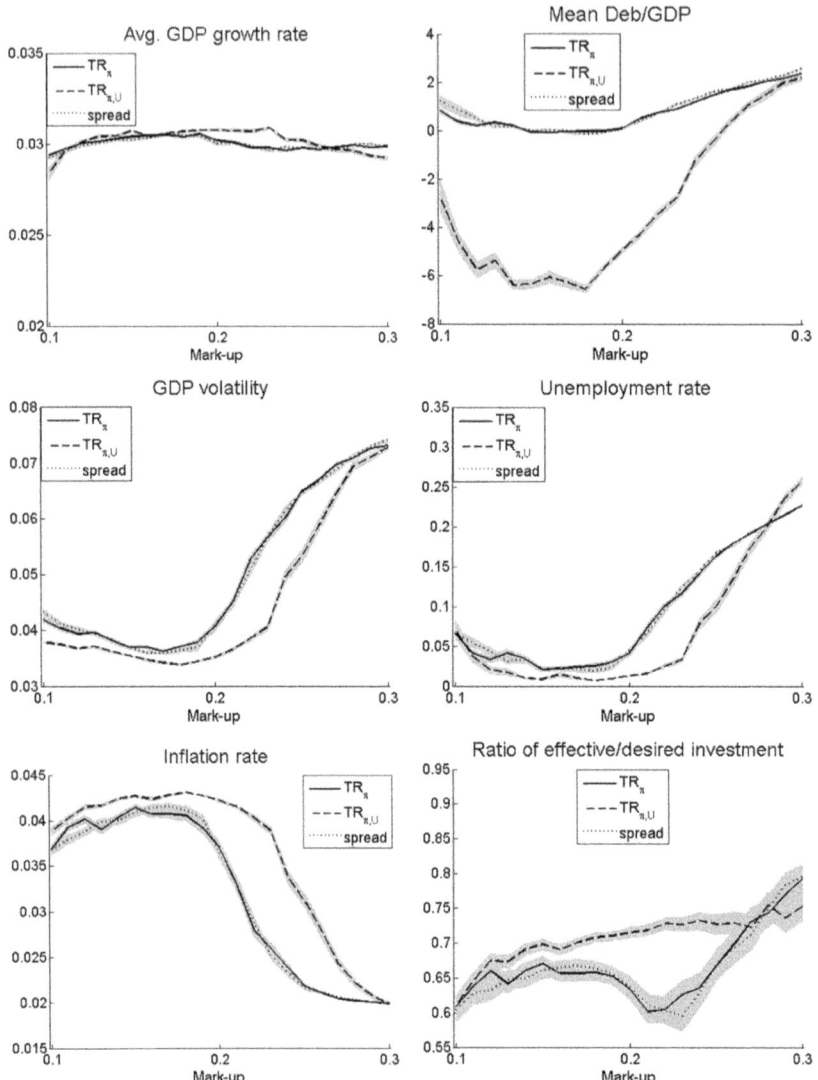

Figure 17 Monetary policy experiments (Dosi et al., 2015). Confidence-interval bands are shown in a lighter colour and are computed as plus or minus two Monte Carlo standard errors.

'conservative' one for every level of inequality without leading to inflation spirals (see Figure 17). Which mechanisms are responsible for such dynamics? With a dual-mandate Taylor rule, the banking sector performs better, as the economy is characterised by a higher share of investment projects that are financed and implemented and a lower rate of banking failures. Lower unemployment pushes interest rates up, thus increasing banks' profitability, while tightening firms' constraints to invest. The increase of the interest rate cools down aggregate demand during booms, while improving the net worth of the banks, leading to a higher supply of credit when the economy experiences a downturn.

Finally, the labour-augmented K+S model allows one to account for the evolution of both functional and personal inequality as heterogeneous workers can earn different wages. We find that the negative impact on economic dynamics of 'structural reforms' designed to increase the flexibility of the labour market reflects also in an increase of the profit share and in a higher personal income concentration (see Table 13). This is in line with the recent empirical evidence on the impact of policies to flexibilise the labour market (see, e.g., Hoffmann, Malacrino, & Pistaferri, 2022; Daruich, Di Addario, & Saggio, 2023). Not surprisingly, functional and personal inequalities further increase when fiscal austerity rules are applied to economies characterised by 'Competitive' labour markets.

7.4 Which Policies for Smooth Inclusive Growth?

The results presented in this section using the Schumpeter meeting Keynes models as a laboratory for simulation experiments illustrate how macroeconomic agent-based models are a powerful and flexible tool for policy analysis. In particular, ABMs allow one to jointly test different ensembles of public interventions, for example innovation, industrial, fiscal and monetary policies, as well as market reforms. Moreover, the impact of policies can be studied at different frequencies, taking into account both their effect on business cycles and their influence on growth dynamics. Policy exercises can be conditioned to different institutional scenarios as shown by our experiments with alternative labour market regimes and different levels of income inequality. Naturally, actual decision makers can be effectively involved in the process of the design of macro agent-based models for policy evaluation (Moss, 2008).

The results of the battery of policy exercises carried out with the K+S models exploit its capability to bridge Schumpeterian theories of technology-driven economic growth with Keynesian theories of demand generation. First, innovation and industrial policies affect both the long- and short-run performance of the economy. However, such policies tuning the 'Schumpeterian engine' are not sufficient to maintain the economy on a high-growth/near full-employment path. Indeed, the endogenous innovation engine is able to do that only in the presence of a 'Keynesian' demand-generating engine, which requires a policy mix comprising (i) an unconstrained fiscal policy, where automatic stabilisers are free to dampen business cycle fluctuations; (ii) a monetary policy targeting both price and employment stability; (iii) 'rigid' labour market institutions (strict firing rules, minimum wage, etc.). Such a policy combination is able to achieve lower unemployment and output volatility *cum* higher productivity and GDP growth.

More generally, our results dispose of the traditional dichotomy between variables impacting the long run (typically, 'supply-side' technology-related changes) and variables with a short-term effect (traditional demand-related variables). On the contrary, technological innovations appear to exert their effects at all frequencies. Conversely, Keynesian demand-management policies do not only contribute to reduce output volatility and unemployment rates, but they affect also long-run growth rates insofar as they contribute to 'delock' the economy from the stagnant growth trajectory, which is indeed one of the possible emergent meta-stable states linked to the structural characteristics of the economy such as functional income inequality. In that, the policy analysis exercises carried out with the K+S models are well in tune with the mentioned empirical evidence showing the ubiquitous presence of hysteresis in macroeconomic dynamics (Dosi et al., 2018a; Cerra et al., 2023).

8 A Brief Discussion on the Future of Macroeconomics by Way of a Conclusion

In a visionary note, Frank Hahn (1991), indeed one of the founding fathers of General Equilibrium theory, was very pessimistic about current theorising in economics:

> Thus we have seen economists abandoning attempts to understand the central question of our subject, namely: how do decentralized choices interact and perhaps get coordinated in favor of a theory according to which an economy is to be understood as the outcome of the maximization of a representative agent's utility over an infinite future? Apart from purely theoretical objections it is clear that this sort of thing heralds the decadence of endeavor just as clearly as Trajan's column heralded the decadence of Rome. It is the last twitch and gasp of a dying method. It rescues rational choice by ignoring every one of the questions pressing for attention. (Hahn, 1991, pp. 47–48)

But he indicates a route for economics for the next hundred years:

> Instead of theorems we shall need simulations, instead of simple transparent axioms there looms the likelihood of psychological, sociological and historical postulates. ... In this respect the signs are that the subject will return to its Marshallian affinities to biology. Evolutionary theories are beginning to flourish, and they are not the sort of theories we have had hitherto. ... But wildly complex systems need simulating. (Hahn, 1991, p. 49)

This moment is now. The Great Recession has prompted a debate about the state of macroeconomic theory, and standard DSGE models have been fiercely criticised by an increasing number of economists for their flaws, which, we believe, are so deep that they cannot be cured. At the same time, agent-based macroeconomics has blossomed naturally, accounting for all the economics problems that require heterogeneity and interactions, such as technical and structural change, inequality, financial intermediation, and so on.

This Element has shown how the *Keynes meeting Schumpeter family of macro agent-based models* is a credible alternative to discredited DSGE models. The K+S models are indeed able to pair Schumpeterian processes of innovation and creative destruction with Keynesian demand-coordination dynamics. In doing so, the approach is able to account for endogenous growth and business cycles punctuated by crises. Beyond accounting for such emergent properties, the K+S models are able to reproduce a rich list of macro and micro stylised facts. Different combinations of policies have been tested, revealing the strong profound complementarities between Schumpeterian innovation policies and Keynesian ones. The results produced by the K+S models unequivocally show the necessity of integrated macroeconomic models to fully grasp the evolution of capitalist economies, in line with the remarks of Solow (2005) and the recent empirical evidence on hysteresis (Cerra et al., 2023).

The generative potentiality of the family of Schumpeter meeting Keynes models – and more generally by macro agent-based models – is shown by the streams of recent works. Here are a few examples.

Concerning the very behavioural foundation, the impact on macroeconomic dynamics of different forms of heterogeneous and boundedly rational expectations is studied in Dosi et al. (2020a). Simulation results show that fast and frugal heuristics (Gigerenzer & Brighton, 2009) are 'rational' responses in complex evolving economies, outperforming OLS-leaning expectations which spur the instability of the system.

The family of K+S models has also expanded along three complementary directions.

In the first direction, we have begun to tackle one of the fundamental questions which have puzzled the economic discipline since at least Ricardo, namely, under what conditions the jab-generation effect of technical progress, – basically associated with the introduction of new products and of the price reduction of existing ones –, compensates the labour-shedding effects productivity enhancements (Dosi et al., 2022).

Second, we have begun to explore the impact of labour market institutions, and in particular the presence or absence of unions, upon the dynamics of wages, inequalities, and, more generally, the whole economy (Dosi et al., 2021; Dosi et al., 2024).

In the third line of research, we have started studying the co-evolution of climate and economic dynamics. More specifically, we have expanded the K+S model: (i) introducing an energy sector populated by heterogenous green and dirty plants, (ii) accounting for greenhouse gas emissions of firms, and (iii) studying the impact of microeconomic climate shocks. With the new Dystopian Schumpeter meeting Keynes model (Lamperti et al., 2018 and 2020), we find that, in the absence of any climate policy, the climate impacts have catastrophic effects on economic dynamics. Such shocks are magnified by the financial system (Lamperti et al., 2019). At the same time, command and control and green industrial policies are able to decarbonise the economy while preserving sustainable growth (Wieners et al., 2024).

And there are quite a few domains still awaiting to be addressed within this art form. Just to name a few: (i) open economies, and more generally, multi-countries and multi-industries set-ups with flows of goods and finance (see Dosi, Roventini, & Russo, 2019, 2020, for the first attempts); (ii) more sophisticated accounts for the (endogenous) dynamics of income distribution, and role of that in conflict among social groups and classes; (iii) opening up the 'organisational blackbox' and the dynamics therein. And there are many others.

A particularly challenging issue concerns the relationship between high-dimensional phenomenologically rich models like the K+S ones, and much simpler lower-dimensional models on the functional links between unemployment, income distribution, and capital accumulation (see also Dosi, Usula, & Virgillito, 2024) or models of 'multiplier-accelerator' of Keynesian flavour such as Pasinetti (1974). Our conjecture is that the two *genres* may be highly complementary in that the latter can be instrumental in deriving analytical predictions (*not forecasts!*) from relatively simple functional hypotheses, while the former are crucial in exploring the domains of their applicability. In between lies a huge field for statistical analyses, both on actual historical data and simulated ones. The 'Phillips curve' mentioned earlier is a good case to illustrate the point. Under what institutional set-ups does it emerge, both in the real world and in the simulated one? And similar questions apply to other purported 'laws of motion' such as the 'accelerator', the 'Verdoorn–Kaldor law', and so on, as well as, of course, debunking pure figments of imagination such as the AS and AD curves.

Moreover, a lot more exploration is required of the policy side. So, as an example, Dosi et al. (2023) assess with a K+S model different types of direct and indirect innovation policies, taking also into account their impact on the public debt. They find that all policies improve productivity and GDP growth, but the best outcomes are achieved by active discretionary state policies, which are also able to crowd-in private investment and have positive hysteresis effects on growth dynamics.

If the foregoing developments suggest that the Dark Age of macroeconomics (Krugman, 2011) is perhaps approaching its end, what prevents agent-based models from becoming the standard way of theorising in macroeconomics? There are some reasons that are theoretical and others that are 'political'.

On the *theory side*, it is certainly true that, as the old adage goes, no matter how badly a theory performs, 'you need a model to replace another one'. However, the alternative macros – indeed more than one! – are already here. What are then the stumbling blocks?

First, as we have been arguing, over roughly the last half a century economics has undergone a thorough 'anthropomorphisation' of models. Nowadays, having a 'structural model' at whatever level of observation entails deriving empirical properties from 'first principles', that is, from whatever is axiomatic on max (something) under some arbitrary constraints. This has trickled down to common language and has merged with a wider *laissez-faire* ideology. So, in everyday discourse, 'markets are optimistic, or nervous, or worried ...'. It is a humanised version of the rational-expectation-based representative agent story, which normatively has far-reaching ideological implications on the predominance of 'incentive', which is well beyond this discussion.[63] Of course, fifty years ago and more, this was not at all the normative. So, for example, Bob Solow and Luigi Pasinetti were debating, often bitterly, on the dynamics of the relative factor intensities, with Bob S. making propositions on the sign of the change based on some property of the purported production function and Luigi P. questioning that very property. Neither one would have dreamed of nesting their argument on what either 'Mr. Market', or, even less so, 'Dr. Doe' would have done! In doing so, however, Solow (take him as the persona of the American reasonable Keynesian growth analyst) took too lightly the 'microfoundation challenge' and the problems stemming from aggregation and from the lack of micro–macro isophormism, while at the opposite extreme, Luigi P. (with many economists of genuinely 'Classical' inspiration) always rejected the very notion of microfoundations, exclusively focusing on *laws of motion* at the system level. The ABM perspective, proposed here, accepts the microfoundation challenge, but fully acknowledges the lack of isomorphism, *More is different, and interactions naturally entail complexity and emergence.*

---

[63] As we discussed at more length in Dosi and Roventini (2016), this way of theorising has reached ridiculous levels when economists develop models of e.g. rational lovemaking, but even worse, criminal ones, when dynamic models of torture are shamelessly derived to compute the optimal level of punishment!

There is no hope of evincing 'anthropomorphism' at all costs, thus shrinking macroeconomics to the micro; but far all the other perspectives, a great challenge indeed is to ground explanations as far away as possible from 'what I think the agent would do in these circumstances'.

Granted that, *second, economies* are *complex* and *evolving* systems. One thing is *complexity*, a distinct one its *evolution*. Boiling spaghetti entails a non-linear system with a few phase transitions. Even more complex are markets with changing networks of interactions. Already the search of possible 'laws of motion' in the latter system is a tall task. However, *evolution is more complex* still: it entails the appearance of new technologies, new entities, new behaviours, along the dynamic paths of a system which would not have been possible from the start. Microprocessors, or the internet, or cars would not have been possible even in principle in the Stone Age! And thus, more technically, the dynamics of evolution cannot be squeezed into finite-state Markov processes. So far, agent-based models have been more concerned with microfounded complexity than with evolution, while too many evolutionary models have taken for granted some simple micro-macro mapping (inspired by one of our major roots, namely Nelson & Winter, 1982). The challenge which some of us have tried to address concerns indeed merging the two domains of analysis.

But, *third,* how does one do it? Any simple aggregative model is bound to fall short of it. Rather, as argued at greater length in Dosi and Virgillito (2017), one should start the dynamic properties of the system in order to derive its coordination properties. We call it jokingly 'the bicycle theorem': in order to stand up you need to keep cycling!

Granted all that, we think that the major obstacle which slows down the success of agent-based macroeconomics has nothing to do with providing better models with higher explanatory power, but has to do with the current norms in the economic profession of what is acceptable and 'scientific', and of what is not in the mainstream.[64] Indeed, the editors of the top journals act as gatekeepers, defending the pure orthodoxy grounded on DSGE models and, more generally, on neoclassical economics. Moreover, the tyranny of the top-five journals regulating placements and tenures in the US university job market does not push young economists to be creative and experiment with new methodologies, but rather rewards careerism, professional incest, and clientelism (Heckman & Moktan, 2020). Max Planck is famously reported to have said that old paradigms disappear with the death of their old proponents. Nowadays, this no longer applies: top journals reproduce and amplify the orthodoxy. (Zombies

---

[64] Romer (2016) also contains a deep discussion on why 'post-real' macroeconomics has emerged and why the current norms in the economic profession make it difficult to jettison.

can be a form of conservatism!) Most young researchers do not dare to go out of their way, but rather please editors and add a minor variation to the paradigm in order to get a position or tenure. Most likely, many Big Ones of the last century, from Keynes to the Arrow tradition, to Nelson, Chandler, C. Freeman, Hirschman, Landes, Winter, Hahn, Pasinetti, Kaldor, and even Bob Solow would not have got a respectable position nowadays![65] (Question to the younger generations: how many names do you recognise in this list?)

What can be done, then? We think that *first* we should keep on nurturing agent-based macroeconomics with outstanding new research, trying also to cooperate with central banks and international institutions and the civil society. In that, we should improve the transparency and reproducibility of agent-based models, possibly sharing a common, evolving set of rules concerning agents' behaviour and a standardised protocol on how to design and empirically validate macroeconomic ABMs.

Second, we must keep on pushing a critical discussion about publications and careers in macroeconomics in the vein of Heckman and Moktan (2020). For this reason, the authors of this Element have worked together with Martin Guzman, Joe Stiglitz, and Marica Virgillito to publish a new outlet for macroeconomic research: the special yearly issue of *Industrial and Corporate Change Macro & Development* (Dosi & Stiglitz, 2021). Still, as we write, there are a few journals in which ABM scholars can publish, with varying degrees of difficulty.[66] For sure, the young researchers face a trade-off between easiness in academic success and pursuit of the 'truth'. Taking the route we suggest is likely to imply a near-zero probability to be published in the top-five.

To (marginally) alleviate the foregoing trade-offs, one of us (G. D.) has recently published a manual to provide the foundations of complex evolving economies (Dosi, 2023) for graduate students.

Third, the ABM perspective must be considered in its evolutionary dimension. Maybe macroeconomics itself is a complex system that sooner or later will self-organise to a new state after an abrupt transition. For sure, one might contemplate a bifurcation similar to the one out of 'moral philosophy' two centuries ago. At that time, it was 'science' searching out of theological thought. This might be the case again now.

---

[65] Nowadays, even Nobel laureates in economics do not have access to top macroeconomic journals if they submit theoretical papers which are not aligned with orthodoxy.

[66] An almost exhaustive list includes the *Journal of Economic Dynamics & Control, Journal of Economic Behavior & Organization, Journal of Evolutionary Economics, Economic Inquiry, Structural Change and Economic Dynamics, Economic Modelling, Macroeconomic Dynamics, Journal of Financial Stability, Journal of Economic Interaction and Coordination, Computational Economics, Italian Economic Journal*.

Appendix A
Parameterizations

Table A.1 Benchmark parameters of the baseline K+S model.

Description	Symbol	Value
Number of firms in capital-goods industry	F_1	50
Number of firms in consumption-goods industry	F_2	200
R&D investment propensity	ν	0.04
R&D allocation to innovative search	ξ	0.50
Firm search capabilities parameters	$\zeta_{1,2}$	0.30
Beta distribution parameters (innovation process)	(α_1, β_1)	(3,3)
Beta distribution support (innovation process)	$[\underline{x}_1, \bar{x}_1]$	$[-0.15, 0.15]$
New-customer sample parameter	γ	0.50
Consumption-goods firm initial mark-up	$\bar{\mu}(0)$	0.30
Capital-goods firm mark-up rule	μ_1	0.04
Desired inventories	ι	0.10
Payback period	b	3
"Physical" scrapping age	η	20
Mark-up coefficient	υ	0.04
Competitiveness weights	$\omega_{1,2}$	1
Replicator dynamics coefficient	χ	1
Maximum debt/sales ratio	Λ	2
Beta distribution parameters (capital-goods entrants technology)	(α_2, β_2)	$(2,4)$
Uniform distribution supports (consumption-goods entrant capital)	$[\phi_1, \phi_2]$	$[0.10, 0.90]$
Uniform distribution supports (entrant stock of liquid assets)	$[\phi_3, \phi_4]$	$[0.10, 0.90]$
Wage indexation to productivity	ψ_1	1
Wage indexation to inflation and unemployment	$\psi_{2,3}$	0.05
Unemployment subsidy rate	φ	0.40
Tax rate	tr	0.10
Interest Rate	r	0.01

Table A.2 Benchmark parameters of the credit and labour extensions of the K+S model.

Description	Symbol	Value
Bond interest rate mark-up	μ^{bonds}	−0.33
Shape parameter of bank client distribution	$pareto_a$	0.08
Bank capital adequacy rate	τ^b	0.08
Capital buffer adjustment parameter	β	1
Inflation adjustment parameter ($TR_{pi}, TR_{\pi,U}$)	γ_π	1.10
Unemployment adjustment parameter ($TR_{pi}, TR_{\pi,U}$)	γ_U	0, 1.10
Target inflation rate	π^T	0.02
Fiscal rule max deficit to GDP (SGP, FC)	def_{rule}	0.03
Labour queue parameter	ϖ	0
Wage indexation to aggregate productivity	ψ_4	0.50
Wage indexation to firm productivity	ψ_5	0.50
Minimum wage indexation to productivity	ψ_6	1

Table A.3 Policy experiments parameters.

	Experiment	Model	Case	Parameter values
E1	Search capabilities	Dosi, Fagiolo, & Roventini (2010)	low	$\zeta_1 = 0.1, \zeta_2 = 0.1$
			high	$\zeta_1 = 0.5, \zeta_2 = 0.5$
E2	Technological opportunities	Dosi, Fagiolo, & Roventini (2010)	low	$\alpha_1 = 2.7, \beta_1 = 3.3$
			high	$\alpha_1 = 3.3, \beta_1 = 2.7$
E3	Patents	Dosi, Fagiolo, & Roventini (2010)	length	12 periods without imitation
			breadth	12 periods without imitation; no innovation close to other firms' technology (range 0.01)
E4	Entrants' productivity	Dosi, Fagiolo, & Roventini (2010)	low	$\alpha_2 = 1.8, \beta_2 = 4.4$
			high	$\alpha_2 = 2.2, \beta_2 = 3.6$
E5	Market selection	Dosi, Fagiolo, & Roventini (2010)	weak	$\chi = 0.95$
			strong	$\chi = 1.05$
E6	Antitrust	Dosi, Fagiolo, & Roventini (2010)	weak	$\max f_j = 75\%$
			strong	$\max f_j = 50\%$
E7	Schumpeterian regime	Dosi, Fagiolo, & Roventini (2010)	pure	$tr = 0, \varphi = 0$
			strong	$tr = 0, \varphi = 0, \alpha_1 = 3.3, \beta_1 = 2.7, \zeta_{1,2} = 0.50$
E8	Fiscal policy stabilizers	Dosi, Fagiolo, & Roventini (2010)	(range)	$tr \in [0.05, 0.2], \varphi \in [0.2, 0.8]$
E9	Fiscal rules	Dosi et al. (2015)	SGP	$def_{rule} = 0.03$
			SGP_{ec}	$def_{rule} = 0.03$, suspended if $\Delta GDP < 0$
E10	Labour market reforms	Dosi et al., (2017, 2019)	(scenario)	Fordist vs. Competive
E11	Monetary policy	Dosi et al. (2015)	(range)	$\gamma_\pi = 1.1, \gamma_U = 0$ or 1.1
E12	Income distribution	Dosi et al. (2013, 2015)	(range)	$\bar{\mu} \in [0.10; 0.40]$

References

Aghion, P., Angeletos, G.-M., Banerjee, A., & Manova, K. (2010). Volatility and growth: Credit constraints and the composition of investment. *Journal of Monetary Economics, 57*, 246–265.

Aghion, P., Askenazy, P., Berman, N., Cette, G., & Eymard, L. (2008). Credit constraints and the cyclicality of R&D investment: Evidence from France. *Journal of the European Economic Association, 10*, 1001–1024.

Aghion, P., Blundell, R., Griffith, R., Howitt, P., & Prantl, S. (2009). The effects of entry on incumbent innovation and productivity. *The Review of Economics and Statistics, 91*, 20–32.

Aghion, P., Hemous, D., & Kharroubi, E. (2014). Cyclical fiscal policy, credit constraints, and industry growth. *Journal of Monetary Economics, 62*, 41–58.

Aghion, P., & Howitt, P. (1992). A model of growth through creative destruction. *Econometrica, 60*, 323–351.

Aghion, P., & Howitt, P. (2007). Appropriate growth policy: A unifying framework. *Journal of the European Economic Association, 4*, 269–314.

Akerlof, G. A. (2002). Behavioral macroeconomics and macroeconomic behavior. *American Economic Review, 92*, 411–433.

Akerlof, G. A. (2007). The missing motivation in macroeconomics. *American Economic Review, 97*, 5–36.

Akerlof, G. A., & Shiller, R. J. (2009). *Animal spirits: How human psychology drives the economy, and why it matters for global capitalism*. Princeton University Press.

Akerlof, G. A., & Yellen, J. L. (1985). A near-rational model of the business cycles, with wage and price inertia. *Quarterly Journal of Economics, 100*, 823–838.

Albert, R., & Barabasi, A. L. (2002). Statistical mechanics of complex networks. *Reviews of Modern Physics, 4*, 47–97.

Alfarano, S., Lux, T., & Wagner, F. (2005). Estimation of agent-based models: The case of an asymmetric herding model. *Computational Economics, 26*, 19–49.

Anderson, P. W. (1972). More is different. *Science, 177*, 393–396.

Anufriev, M., Assenza, T., Hommes, C., & Massaro, D. (2013). Interest rate rules and macroeconomic stability under heterogeneous expectations. *Macroeconomic Dynamics, 17*, 1574–1604.

References

Anufriev, M., Bao, T., & Tuinstra, J. (2016). Microfoundations for switching behavior in heterogeneous agent models: An experiment. *Journal of Economic Behavior & Organization, 129*, 74–99.

Ascari, G., Fagiolo, G., & Roventini, A. (2015). Fat-tail distributions and business-cycle models. *Macroeconomic Dynamics, 19*, 465–476.

Ascari, G., & Ropele, T. (2009). Trend inflation, Taylor principle, and indeterminacy. *Journal of Money, Credit and Banking, 41*, 1557–1584.

Ashraf, Q., Gershman, B., & Howitt, P. (2017). Banks, market organization, and macroeconomic performance: An agent-based computational analysis. *Journal of Economic Behavior & Organization, 135*, 143–180.

Assenza, T., Delli Gatti, D., & Grazzini, J. (2015). Emergent dynamics of a macroeconomic agent based model with capital and credit. *Journal of Economic Dynamics and Control, 50*, 5–28.

Atkinson, A. B., Piketty, T., & Saez, E. (2011). Top incomes in the long run of history. *Journal of Economic Literature, 49*, 3–71.

Ausloos, M., Miskiewicz, J., & Sanglier, M. (2004). The durations of recession and prosperity: Does their distribution follow a power or an exponential law? *Physica A: Statistical Mechanics and Its Applications, 339*, 548–558.

Bak, P., Chen, K., Scheinkman, J. A., & Woodford, M. (1992). Aggregate fluctuations from independent sectoral shocks: Self-organize criticality (Working Paper No. 4241). National Bureau of Economic Research.

Balint, T., Lamperti, F., Mandel, A., Napoletano, M., Roventini, A., & Sapio, S. (2017). Complexity and the economics of climate change: A survey and a look forward. *Ecological Economics, 138*, 252–265.

Barde, S. (2016). A practical, accurate, information criterion for nth order Markov processes. *Computational Economics, 50*, 1–44.

Bargigli, L., Riccetti, L., Russo, A., & Gallegati, M. (2020, April). Network calibration and metamodeling of a financial accelerator agent based model. *Journal of Economic Interaction and Coordination, 15*, 413–440.

Bartelsman, E., & Doms, M. (2000). Understanding productivity: Lessons from longitudinal microdata. *Journal of Economic Literature, 38*, 569–594.

Bartelsman, E., Scarpetta, S., & Schivardi, F. (2005). Comparative analysis of firm demographics and survival: Evidence from micro-level sources in OECD countries. *Industrial and Corporate Change, 14*, 365–391.

Battiston, S., Farmer, D. J., Flache, A. et al. (2016). Complexity theory and financial regulation. *Science, 351*, 818–819.

Bellone, F., Musso, P., Nesta, L., & Quéré, M. (2008). Market selection along the firm life cycle. *Industrial and Corporate Change, 17*, 753–777.

Benhabib, J., Schmitt-Grohé, S., & Uribe, M. (2001). The perils of Taylor rules. *Journal of Economic Theory, 96*, 40–69.

Bernanke, B. S. (2004). *The great moderation.* Available at www.federalreserve.gov/BOARDDOCS/SPEECHES/2004/20040220/default.htm

Bernanke, B. S. (2002). On Milton Friedman's ninetieth birthday. In *Remarks by Governor Ben S. Bernanke at the Conference to Honor Milton Friedman, University of Chicago, Chicago, Illinois November 8, 2002.* https://www.federalreserve.gov/BOARDDOCS/SPEECHES/2002/20021108/

Bernanke, B. S., Gertler, M., & Gilchrist, S. (1999). The financial accelerator in a quantitative business cycle framework. In J. B. Taylor & M. Woodford (eds.), *Handbook of macroeconomics* (pp. 1341–1393). Elsevier.

Beyer, A., & Farmer, R. E. A. (2004). On the indeterminacy of New-Keynesian economics (Working Paper Series No. 323). European Central Bank.

BIS. (1999). Capital requirements and bank behaviour: The impact of the Basel Accord (Working Papers No. 1). Bank for International Settlements.

Bloomquist, K. M., & Koehler, M. (2015). A large-scale agent-based model of taxpayer reporting compliance. *Journal of Artificial Societies and Social Simulation, 18,* 20.

Boivin, J., Kiley, M. T., & Mishkin, F. S. (2010). How has the monetary transmission mechanism evolved over time? In B. M. Friedman & M. Woodford (eds.), *Handbook of monetary economics* (pp. 369–422). Elsevier.

Bookstaber, R. (2017). *The end of theory: Financial crises, the failure of economics, and the sweep of human interaction.* Princeton University Press.

Bookstaber, R., & Paddrik, M. (2015). An agent-based model for crisis liquidity dynamics (Working Paper No. 15-18). Office of Financial Research.

Bottazzi, G., & Secchi, A. (2003). Common properties and sectoral specificities in the dynamics of U.S. manufacturing firms. *Review of Industrial Organization, 23,* 217–32.

Bottazzi, G., & Secchi, A. (2006). Explaining the distribution of firm growth rates. *RAND Journal of Economics, 37,* 235–256.

Branch, W. A., & McGough, B. (2011). Monetary policy and heterogeneous agents. *Economic Theory, 47,* 365–393.

Braun-Munzinger, K., Liu, Z., & Turrell, A. (2016). An agent-based model of dynamics in corporate bond trading (Staff Working Paper No. 592). Bank of England.

Brock, W. A., Durlauf, S. N., Nason, J. M., & Rondina, G. (2007). Simple versus optimal rules as guides to policy. *Journal of Monetary Economics, 54,* 1372–1396.

Brock, W. A., & Durlauf, S. N. (2001). Interactions-based models. In J. Heckman & E. Leamer (Eds.), *Handbook of econometrics.* North Holland.

Brock, W. A., & Hommes, C. (1997). A rational route to randomness. *Econometrica*, *65*, 1059–1095.

Burns, A. F., & Mitchell, W. C. (1946). *Measuring business cycles*. National Bureau of Economic Research.

Caballero, R. J. (1999). Aggregate investment. In J. Taylor & M. Woodford (Eds.), *Handbook of macroeconomics*. Elsevier Science.

Caballero, R. J. (2010). Macroeconomics after the crisis: Time to deal with the pretense-of-knowledge syndrome. *Journal of Economic Perspectives*, *24*, 85–102.

Caiani, A., Godin, A., Caverzasi, E., Gallegati, M., Kinsella, S., & Stiglitz, J. (2016). Agent based-stock flow consistent macroeconomics: Towards a benchmark model. *Journal of Economic Dynamics & Control*, *69*, 375–408.

Canova, F. (2008). How much structure in empirical models? In T. Mills & K. Patterson (Eds.), *Palgrave handbook of econometrics* (Vol. 2, Applied Econometrics). Palgrave Macmillan.

Canova, F., & Sala, L. (2009). Back to square one: Identification issues in DSGE models. *Journal of Monetary Economics*, *56*, 431–449.

Canzoneri, M., Collard, F., Dellas, H., & Diba, B. (2016). Fiscal multipliers in recessions. *The Economic Journal*, *126*, 75–108.

Carro, A., Hinterschweiger, M., Uluc, A., & Farmer, J. D. (2022, 07). Heterogeneous effects and spillovers of macroprudential policy in an agent-based model of the UK housing market. *Industrial and Corporate Change*, *32*, 386–432.

Cassidy, J. (2009). *How markets fail*. London/New York Allen Lane.

Castaldi, C., & Dosi, G. (2009). The patterns of output growth of firms and countries: Scale invariances and scale specificities. *Empirical Economics*, *37*, 475–495.

Caverzasi, E., & Russo, A. (2018). Toward a new microfounded macroeconomics in the wake of the crisis. *Industrial and Corporate Change*, *27*, 999–1014.

Caves, R. (1998). Industrial organization and new findings on the turnover and mobility of firms. *Journal of Economic Literature*, *36*, 1947–1982.

Cerra, V., Fatás, A., & Saxena, S. C. (2023, March). Hysteresis and business cycles. *Journal of Economic Literature*, *61*, 181–225.

Chan-Lau, J. A. (2017). Abba: An agent-based model of the banking system (IMF Working Paper No. 17/136).

Chari, V. V., Kehoe, P. J., & McGrattan, E. R. (2009) New Keynesian models are not yet useful for policy analysis. *American Economic Journal: Macroeconomics*, *1*, 242–266.

Christiano, L. G., Motto, R., & Rostagno, M. (2013). Risk shocks. *American Economic Review, 104*, 27–65.

Ciarli, T., Lorentz, A., Valente, M., & Savona, M. (2019). Structural changes and growth regimes. *Journal of Evolutionary Economics, 29*, 119–176.

Cimoli, M., Dosi, G., Maskus, K. E., Okediji, R. L., Reichman, J. H., & Stiglitz, J. E. (Eds.). (2014). *Intellectual property rights: Legal and economic challenges for development.* Oxford University Press.

Cincotti, S., Raberto, M., & Teglio, A. (2010). Credit money and macroeconomic instability in the agent-based model and simulator eurace. *Economics: The Open-Access, Open-Assessment E-Journal, 4*(2010-26).

Clarida, R., Galí, J., & Gertler, M. (1999). The science of monetary policy: A new Keynesian perspective. *Journal of Economic Literature, 37*, 1661–1707.

Cogley, T., & Nason, J. M. (1993). Impulse dynamics and propagation mechanisms in a real business cycle model. *Economic Letters, 43*, 77–81.

Coibion, O., & Gorodnichenko, Y. (2015). Information rigidity and the expectations formation process: A simple framework and new facts. *American Economic Review, 105*, 2644–2678.

Colander, D., Folmer, H., Haas, A., et al. (2009). *The financial crisis and the systemic failure of academic economics* (Tech. Rep.). 98th Dahlem Workshop.

Cooper, R. W., & John, A. (1988). Coordinating coordination failures in Keynesian models. *Quarterly Journal of Economics, 103*, 441–463.

Curdia, V., Del Negro, M., & Greenwald, D. (2014). Rare shocks, great recessions. *Journal of Applied Econometrics, 29*, 1031–1052.

Curdia, V., & Woodford, M. (2010). Credit spreads and monetary policy. *Journal of Money, Credit and Banking, 42*, 3–35.

Curdia, V., & Woodford, M. (2011). The central-bank balance sheet as an instrument of monetary policy. *Journal of Monetary Economics, 58*, 54–79.

Curdia, V., & Woodford, M. (2016). Credit frictions and optimal monetary policy. *Journal of Monetary Economics, 84*, 30–65.

Cyert, R. M., & March, J. G. (1992). *A behavioral theory of the firm* (2nd ed.). Blackwell Business: Oxford.

Daruich, D., Di Addario, S., & Saggio, R. (2023). The effects of partial employment protection reforms: Evidence from Italy. *The Review of Economic Studies, 90*, 2880–2942.

Da Silva, M. A., & Tadeu Lima, G. (2015). Combining monetary policy and prudential regulation: An agent-based modeling approach (Working paper No. 394). Banco Central do Brasil.

Dawid, H., & Delli Gatti, D. (2018). Agent-based macroeconomics. In C. Hommes & B. LeBaron (Eds.), *Handbook of computational economics, volume iv*. Elsevier.

Dawid, H., Gemkow, S., Harting, P., van der Hoog, S., & Neugart, M. (2014a). Agent-based macroeconomic modeling and policy analysis: The eurace@unibi model. In S.-H. Chen & M. Kaboudan (Eds.), *Handbook on computational economics and finance*. Oxford University Press.

Dawid, H., Harting, P., & Neugart, M. (2014b). Economic convergence: Policy implications from a heterogeneous agent model. *Journal of Economic Dynamics & Control, 44*, 54–80.

Dawid, H., Harting, P., & Neugart, M. (2018). Cohesion policy and inequality dynamics: Insights from a heterogeneous agents macroeconomic model. *Journal of Economic Behavior & Organization, 150*, 220–255.

Dawid, H., Harting, P., van der Hoog, S., & Neugart, M. (2019). Macroeconomics with heterogeneous agent models: Fostering transparency, reproducibility and replication. *Journal of Evolutionary Economics, 29*, 467–538.

Debreu, G. (1974). Excess demand function. *Journal of Mathematical Economics, 1*, 15–23.

De Grauwe, P. (2012). Booms and busts in economic activity: A behavioral explanation. *Journal of Economic Behavior & Organization, 83*, 484–501.

Del Boca, A., Galeotti, M., Himmelberg, C. P., & Rota, P. (2008). Investment and time to plan and build: A comparison of structures vs. equipment in a panel of italian firms. *Journal of the European Economic Association, 6*, 864–889.

Delli Gatti, D., Di Guilmi, C., Gaffeo, E., Giulioni, G., Gallegati, M., & Palestrini, A. (2005). A new approach to business fluctuations: Heterogeneous interacting agents, scaling laws and financial fragility. *Journal of Economic Behavior & Organization, 56*, 489–512.

Delli Gatti, D., & Grazzini, J. (2020). Rising to the challenge: Bayesian estimation and forecasting techniques for macroeconomic agent based models. *Journal of Economic Behavior & Organization, 178*, 875–902.

De Long, J. B. (2000). The triumph of monetarism? *Journal of Economic Perspectives, 14*, 83–94.

Di Guilmi, C., Gallegati, M., & Ormerod, P. (2004). Scaling invariant distributions of firms' exit in OECD countries. *Physica A: Statistical and Theoretical Physics, 334*, 267–273.

Dilaver, O., Jump, R., & Levine, P. (2018). Agent-based macroeconomics and dynamic stochastic general equilibrium models: Where do we go from here? *Journal of Economic Surveys, 32*, 1134–1159.

Domar, E. D. (1946). Capital expansion, rate of growth, and employment. *Econometrica, 14,* 137–147.

Doms, M., & Dunne, T. (1998). Capital adjustment patterns in manufacturing plants. *Review Economic Dynamics, 1,* 409–429.

Dosi, G. (2007). Statistical regularities in the evolution of industries: A guide through some evidence and challenges for the theory. In F. Malerba & S. Brusoni (Eds.), *Perspectives on innovation.* Cambridge University Press.

Dosi, G. (2012). Economic coordination and dynamics: Some elements of an alternative 'evolutionary' paradigm (LEM Working Papers Series No. 2012/08). Scuola Superiore Sant'Anna.

Dosi, G. (2014). Introduction. In *Economic organization, industrial dynamics and development.* Edward Elgar.

Dosi, G. (2023). *The foundations of complex evolving economies.* Oxford University Press.

Dosi, G., Fagiolo, G., Napoletano, M., & Roventini, A. (2013). Income distribution, credit and fiscal policies in an agent-based Keynesian model. *Journal of Economic Dynamics & Control, 37,* 1598–1625.

Dosi, G., Fagiolo, G., Napoletano, M., Roventini, A., & Treibich, T. (2015). Fiscal and monetary policies in complex evolving economies. *Journal of Economic Dynamics & Control, 52,* 166–189.

Dosi, G., Fagiolo, G., & Roventini, A. (2006). An evolutionary model of endogenous business cycles. *Computational Economics, 27,* 3–34.

Dosi, G., Fagiolo, G., & Roventini, A. (2008). The microfoundations of business cycles: An evolutionary, multi-agent model. *Journal of Evolutionary Economics, 18,* 413–432.

Dosi, G., Fagiolo, G., & Roventini, A. (2010). Schumpeter meeting Keynes: A policy-friendly model of endogenous growth and business cycles. *Journal of Economic Dynamics & Control, 34,* 1748–1767.

Dosi, G., Faillo, M., & Marengo, L. (2018). Beyond 'bounded rationality': Behaviours and learning in complex evolving worlds (LEM Working Papers Series No. 2018/26). Scuola Superiore Sant'Anna.

Dosi, G., Freeman, C., Nelson, R., Silverberg, G., & Soete, L. (1988). *Technical change and economic theory* (Vol. 988). Pinter.

Dosi, G., Freeman, R. B., Pereira, M. C., Roventini, A., & Virgillito, M. E. (2021). The impact of deunionization on the growth and dispersion of productivity and pay. *Industrial and Corporate Change, 30,* 377–408.

Dosi, G., Lamperti, F., Mazzucato, M., Napoletano, M., & Roventini, A. (2023). Mission-oriented policies and the 'Entrepreneurial State' at work:

An agent-based exploration. *Journal of Economic Dynamics and Control, 151*, 104650.

Dosi, G., Malerba, F., Marsili, O., & Orsenigo, L. (1997). Industrial structures and dynamics: Evidence, interpretations and puzzles. *Industrial and Corporate Change, 6*, 3–24.

Dosi, G., Marengo, L., & Pasquali, C. (2006). How much should society fuel the greed of innovators?: On the relations between appropriability, opportunities and rates of innovation. *Research Policy, 35*, 1110–1121.

Dosi, G., Marsili, O., Orsenigo, L., & Salvatore, R. (1995). Learning, market selection and the evolution of industrial structures. *Small Business Economics, 7*, 411–436.

Dosi, G., Napoletano, M., Roventini, A., Stiglitz, J. E., & Treibich, T. (2020a). Rational heuristics? Expectations and behaviors in evolving economies with heterogenous interacting agents. *Economic Inquiry, 58*, 1487–1516.

Dosi, G., Napoletano, M., Roventini, A., & Treibich, T. (2016a). Micro and macro policies in Keynes+Schumpeter evolutionary models. *Journal of Evolutionary Economics, 27*, 63–90.

Dosi, G., Napoletano M., Roventini A., and Treibich T. (2016b). The short- and long-run damages of fiscal austerity: Keynes beyond Schumpeter. In Stiglitz J. E. and M. Guzman (Eds.), *Contemporary issues in macroeconomics: Lessons from the crisis and beyond.* Palgrave Macmillan.

Dosi, G., Palagi, E., Roventini, A., & Russo, E. (2022). Do patents really foster innovation in the pharmaceutical sector? Results from an evolutionary, agent-based model. *Journal of Economic Behavior & Organization, 212*, 564–589.

Dosi, G., Pereira, M. C., Roventini, A., & Virgillito, M. E. (2017). When more flexibility yields more fragility: The microfoundations of Keynesian aggregate unemployment. *Journal of Economic Dynamics & Control, 81*, 162–186.

Dosi, G., Pereira, M. C., Roventini, A., & Virgillito, M. E. (2018a). Causes and consequences of hysteresis: Aggregate demand, productivity and employment. *Industrial and Corporate Change, 27*, 1015–1044.

Dosi, G., Pereira, M. C., Roventini, A., & Virgillito, M. E. (2018b). The effects of labour market reforms upon unemployment and income inequalities: An agent-based model. *Socio-Economic Review, 16*, 687–720.

Dosi, G., Pereira, M. C., Roventini, A., & Virgillito, M. E. (2019). What if supply-side policies are not enough? The perverse interaction of flexibility and austerity. *Journal of Economic Behavior & Organization, 162*, 360–388.

Dosi, G., Pereira, M. C., Roventini, A., & Virgillito, M. E. (2020b). The labour-augmented K+S model: A laboratory for the analysis of institutional and policy regimes. *EconomiA*, *21*, 160–184.

Dosi, G., Pereira, M. C., Roventini, A., & Virgillito, M. E. (2022). Technological paradigms, labour creation and destruction in a multi-sector agent-based model. *Research Policy*, *51*, 104565.

Dosi, G., Pereira, M. C., Roventini, A., & Virgillito, M. E. (2024). The political economy of complex evolving systems: The case of declining unionization and rising inequalities. In *The economy as a complex evolving system - part iv*. SFI Press.

Dosi, G., Pereira, M. C., & Virgillito, M. E. (2017). On the robustness of the fat-tailed distribution of firm growth rates: A global sensitivity analysis. *Journal of Economic Interaction and Coordination*, *13*, 173–193.

Dosi, G., & Roventini, A. (2016). The irresistible fetish of utility theory: From 'pleasure and pain' to rationalising torture. *Intereconomics*, *51*, 286–287.

Dosi, G., & Roventini, A. (2017). Agent-based macroeconomics and classical political economy: Some Italian roots. *Italian Economic Journal*, *3*, 261–283.

Dosi, G., & Roventini, A. (2019). More is different... and complex! The case for agent-based macroeconomics. *Journal of Evolutionary Economics*, *29*, 1–37.

Dosi, G., Roventini, A., & Russo, E. (2019). Endogenous growth and global divergence in a multi-country agent-based model. *Journal of Economic Dynamics and Control*, *101*, 101–129.

Dosi, G., Roventini, A., & Russo, E. (2020). Public policies and the art of catching up: Matching the historical evidence with a multicountry agent-based model. *Industrial and Corporate Change*, *30*, 1011–1036.

Dosi, G., Sodini, M., & Virgillito, M. E. (2015). Profit-driven and demand-driven investment growth and fluctuations in different accumulation regimes. *Journal of Evolutionary Economics*, *25*, 707–728.

Dosi, G., & Stiglitz, J. E. (2021). Introduction to the first annual special issue on Macro Economics and Development. *Industrial and Corporate Change*, *30*, 269–271.

Dosi, G., Usula, D., & Virgillito, M. E. (2024). Increasing returns and labor markets in a predator–prey model. *Journal of Evolutionary Economics*, *34*, 375–402.

Dosi, G., & Virgillito, M. E. (2017). In order to stand up you must keep cycling: Change and coordination in complex evolving economies. *Structural Change and Economic Dynamics*, *56*, 353–364.

Dosi, G., & Winter, S. G. (2002). Interpreting economic change: Evolution, structures and games. In M. Augier & J. March (Eds.), *The economics of choice, change, and organizations*. Edward Elgar.

Dos Santos, T., & Nakane, M. (2017). Dynamic bank runs: An agent-based approach (Working Paper No. 465). Banco Central do Brasil.

Edelman, G. M., & Gally, J. A. (2001). Degeneracy and complexity in biological systems. *Proceedings of the National Academy of Sciences*, *98*, 13763–13768.

Eggertsson, G. B., & Krugman, P. (2012). Debt, deleveraging, and the liquidity trap: A Fisher-Minsky-Koo approach. *Quarterly Journal of Economics*, *127*, 1469–1513.

Eisner, R. (1972). Components of capital expenditures: Replacement and modernization versus expansion. *The Review of Economics and Statistics*, *54*, 297–305.

Evans, G. W., & Honkapohja, S. (2001). *Learning and expectations in macroeconomics*. Princeton University Press.

Fabiani, S., Druant, M., Hernando, I., Kwapil, C., Landau, B., Loupias, C., Martins, F., Mathä, T., Sabbatini, R., Stahl, H., and Stokman, A. (2006). What firms' surveys tell us about price-setting behavior in the euro area. *International Journal of Central Banking*, *2*, 3–47.

Fagiolo, G., Guerini, M., Lamperti, F., Moneta, A., & Roventini, A. (2017). Validation of agent-based models in economics and finance. In C. Beisbart & N. J. Saam (Eds.), *Computer simulation validation. fundamental concepts, methodological frameworks, philosophical perspectives*. Springer International Publishing.

Fagiolo, G., Napoletano, M., & Roventini, A. (2008). Are output growth-rate distributions fat-tailed? Some evidence from OECD countries. *Journal of Applied Econometrics*, *23*, 639–669.

Fagiolo, G., & Roventini, A. (2012). Macroeconomic policy in DSGE and Agent-Based Models. *Revue de l'OFCE*, *124*, 67–116.

Fagiolo, G., & Roventini, A. (2017). Macroeconomic policy in DSGE and Agent-Based Models redux: New developments and challenges ahead. *Journal of Artificial Societies and Social Simulation*, *20*, 1.

Farmer, D. J., & Foley, D. (2009). The economy needs agent-based modeling. *Nature*, *460*, 685–686.

Farrel, J., & Shapiro, C. (1988). Dynamic competition with switching costs. *RAND Journal of Economics*, *19*, 123–137.

Favero, C. (2007). Model evaluation in macroeconometrics: From early empirical macroeconomic models to DSGE models (Working Paper No. 327). IGIER, Bocconi University.

Feldstein, M., & Foot, D. (1971). The other half of gross investment: Replacement and modernization expenditures. *The Review of Economics and Statistics, 53*, 49–58.

Fernandez-Villaverde, J., & Levintal, O. (2018). Solution methods for models with rare disasters. *Quantitative Economics, 9*, 903–944.

Fitoussi, J.-P. & Saraceno, F. (2010). *Inequality and macroeconomic performance* (Document de Travail No. 2010-13). OFCE.

Fitoussi, J.-P., & Saraceno, F. (2013). European economic governance: the Berlin–Washington consensus. *Cambridge Journal of Economics, 37*, 479–496.

Fogel, K., Morck, R., & Yeung, B. (2008). Big business stability and economic growth: Is what's good for general motors good for america? *Journal of Financial Economics, 89*, 83–108.

Foos, D., Norden, L., & Weber, M. (2010). Loan growth and riskiness of banks. *Journal of Banking and Finance, 34*, 2929–2940.

Forni, M., & Lippi, M. (1997). *Aggregation and the microfoundations of dynamic macroeconomics*. Oxford University Press.

Forni, M., & Lippi, M. (1999). Aggregation of linear dynamic microeconomic models. *Journal of Mathematical Economics, 31*, 131–158.

Friedman, M. (1968). The role of monetary policy. *American Economic Review, 58*, 1–17.

Fukac, M., & Pagan, A. (2006). Issues in adopting DSGE models for use in the policy process (Working Paper No. 10/2006). CAMA.

Fukuyama, F. (1992). *The end of history and the last man*. Penguin.

Gabaix, X. (2014). A sparsity-based model of bounded rationality. *The Quarterly Journal of Economics, 129*, 1661–1710.

Galí, J., & Gertler, M. (2007). Macroeconomic modelling for monetary policy evaluation. *Journal of Economic Perspectives, 21*, 25–46.

Gennaioli, N., Ma, Y., & Shleifer, A. (2015). Expectations and investment. *NBER Macroeconomics Annual, 30*, 379–431.

Gertler, M., & Karadi, P. (2011). A model of unconventional monetary policy. *Journal of Monetary Economics, 58*, 17–34.

Gertler, M., & Kiyotaki, N. (2010). Financial intermediation and credit policy in business cycle analysis. In B. M. Friedman & M. Woodford (Eds.), *Handbook of monetary economics*. North Holland.

Gigerenzer, G. (2007). *Gut feelings: The intelligence of the unconscious*. Viking.

Gigerenzer, G., & Brighton, H. (2009). Homo heuristicus: Why biased minds make better inferences. *Topics in Cognitive Science, 1*, 107–143.

Goodfriend, M. (2007). How the world achieved consensus on monetary policy. *Journal of Economic Perspectives, 21*, 47–68.

Goodhart, C. A. E. (2009). The continuing muddles of monetary theory: A steadfast refusal to face facts. *Economica, 76*, 821–830.

Goodwin, R. M. (1950). A nonlinear theory of the cycle. *Review of Economic Studies, 32*, 316–320.

Goodwin, R. M. (1951). The nonlinear accelerator and the persistence of business cycles. *Econometrica, 19*, 1–17.

Goolsbee, A. (1998). The business cycle, financial performance, and the retirement of capital goods. *Review of Economic Dynamics, 1*, 474–496.

Gourio, F., & Kashyap, A. K. (2007). Investment spikes: New facts and a general equilibrium exploration. *Journal of Monetary Economics, 54*, 1–22.

Grazzini, J., & Richiardi, M. (2015). Estimation of ergodic agent-based models by simulated minimum distance. *Journal of Economic Dynamics & Control Control, 51*, 148–165.

Grazzini, J., Richiardi, M., & Sellad, L. (2013). Indirect estimation of agent-based models: An application to a simple diffusion model. *Complexity Economics, 2*, 25–40.

Grazzini, J., Richiardi, M. G., & Tsionas, M. (2017). Bayesian estimation of agent-based models. *Journal of Economic Dynamics and Control, 77*, 26–47.

Greenwald, B., & Stiglitz, J. (1993a). Financial market imperfections and business cycles. *Quarterly Journal of Economics, 108*, 77–114.

Greenwald, B., & Stiglitz, J. (1993b). New and old Keynesians. *Journal of Economic Perspectives, 7*, 23–44.

Greenwald, B., & Stiglitz, J. (2003). Macroeconomic fluctuations in an economy of Phelps–Winter markets. In P. Aghion, R. Frydman, J. Stiglitz, & M. Woodford (Eds.), *Knowledge, information, and expectations in modern macroeconomics: In honor of Edmund S. Phelps*. Princeton University Press.

Guerini, M., & Moneta, A. (2017). A method for agent-based models validation. *Journal of Economic Dynamics and Control, 82*, 125–141.

Hahn, F. (1991). The next hundred years. *The Economic Journal, 101*, 47–50.

Halaj, G. (2018). Agent-based model of system-wide implications of funding risk (Working Paper Series No. 2121). European Central Bank.

Haldane, A. (2012). *The dog and the frisbee* (central bankers' speeches). BIS.

Haldane, A. G., & Turrell, A. E. (2019). Drawing on different disciplines: macroeconomic agent-based models. *Journal of Evolutionary Economics, 29*, 39–66.

Harcourt, G. C. (2007). The structure of post-Keynesian economics. *History of Economics Review*, *45*, 95–105.

Harcourt, G. C., Karmel, P. H., & Wallace, R. H. (1967). *Economic activity*. Cambridge University Press.

Harrod, R. F. (1939). An essay in dynamic theory. *Economic Journal*, *49*, 14–33.

Heckman, J., & Moktan, S. (2020). Publishing and promotion in economics: The tyranny of the top five. *Journal of Economic Litarature*, *58*, 419–470.

Hendry, D., & Minzon, G. (2010). On the mathematical basis of inter-temporal optimization (Economics Series Working Papers No. 497). University of Oxford.

Hicks, J. R. (1937). Mr. Keynes and the 'Classics': A suggested interpretation. *Econometrica*, *5*, 147–159.

Hoffmann, E. B., Malacrino, D., & Pistaferri, L. (2022). Earnings dynamics and labor market reforms: The Italian case. *Quantitative Economics*, *13*, 1637–1667.

Hommes, C. (2013). *Behavioral Rationality and Heterogeneous Expectations in Complex Economic Systems*. Cambridge University Press.

Hosszu, S., & Mero, B. (2017). An agent based Keynesian model with credit cycles and countercyclical capital buffer (MNB Working Papers No. 5). Magyar Nemzeti Bank.

Howitt, P. (2012). What have central bankers learned from modern macroeconomic theory? *Journal of Macroeconomics*, *34*, 11–22.

Hubbard, G. R. (1998). Capital-market imperfections and investment. *Journal of Economic Literature*, *36*, 193–225.

Jaimovich, N., & Floetotto, M. (2008). Firm dynamics, markup variations, and the business cycle. *Journal of Monetary Economics*, *55*, 1238–1252.

Johansen, S. (2006). Confronting the economic model with the data. In D. Colander (Ed.), *Post Walrasian macroeconomics*. Cambridge University Press.

Juselius, K., & Franchi, M. (2007). Taking a DSGE model to the data meaningfully. *Economics – The Open-Access, Open-Assessment E-Journal*, *1*(4).

Kaldor, N. (1957). A model of economic growth. *The Economic Journal*, *67*, 591–624.

Kaldor, N. (1982). *The scourge of monetarism*. Oxford University Press.

Kaplan, G., Moll, B., & Violante, G. L. (2018). Monetary policy according to Hank. *American Economic Review*, *108*, 697–743.

Kay, J. (2011). *The map is not the territory: An essay on the state of economics*. Institute for New Economic Thinking.

Keynes, J. M. (1921). *Treatise on probability*. Macmillan and Co.

Keynes, J. M. (1936). *The general theory of employment, interest, and money*. Prometheus Books.

Kirman, A. P. (1989). The intrinsic limits of modern economic theory: The emperor has no clothes. *Economic Journal, 99*, 126–39.

Kirman, A. P. (1992). Whom or what does the representative individual represent? *Journal of Economic Perspectives, 6*, 117–136.

Kirman, A. P. (2010a). *Complex economics: Individual and collective rationality*. Routledge.

Kirman, A. P. (2010b). The economic crisis is a crisis for economic theory. *CESifo Economic Studies, 56*, 498–535.

Kirman, A. P. (2014). Is it rational to have rational expectations? *Mind and Society, 13*, 29–48.

Kirman, A. P. (2016). Ants and nonoptimal self-organization: Lessons for macroeconomics. *Macroeconomic Dynamics, 20*, 601–621.

Kirman, A. P., & Vriend, N. J. (2001). Evolving market structure: An ace model of price dispersion and loyalty. *Journal of Economic Dynamics and Control, 25*, 459–502.

Klamer, A. (1984). *The new classical macroeconomics: Conversations with the New Classical economists and their opponents*. Wheatsheaf Books.

Klemperer, P. D. (1987). Markets with customer switching costs. *Quarterly Journal of Economics, 102*, 375–394.

Klemperer, P. D. (1995). Competition when consumers have switching costs: An overview with applications to industrial organization, macroeconomics and international trade. *Review of Economic Studies, 62*, 515–539.

Klevorick, A. K., Levin, R., Nelson, R. R., & Winter, S. G. (1995). On the sources and significance of interindustry differences in technological opportunities. *Research Policy, 24*, 185–205.

Knight, F. (1921). *Risk, uncertainty, and profits*. Chicago University Press.

Krugman, P. (2009). How did economics get it so wrong? *New York Times Magazine* (9), 36–44.

Krugman, P. (2011). The profession and the crisis. *Eastern Economic Journal, 37*, 307–312.

Kumhof, M., & Rancière, R. (2015). Inequality, leverage and crisis. *American Economic Review, 105*, 1217–1245.

Kuznets, S., & Murphy, J. T. (1966). *Modern economic growth: Rate, structure, and spread*. Yale University Press.

Kydland, F. E., & Prescott, E. C. (1982). Time to build and aggregate fluctuations. *Econometrica, 50*, 1345–1370.

Laeven, L., & Valencia, F. (2008). Systemic banking crises: A new database (Working Paper No. WP/08/224). International Monetary Fund.

Lamperti, F. (2018). Empirical validation of simulated models through the GSL-DIV: An illustrative application. *Journal of Economic Interaction and Coordination, 13*, 143–171.

Lamperti, F., Bosetti, V., Roventini, A., and Tavoni M. (2019). The public costs of climate-induced financial instability. *Nature Climate Change, 9*, 829–833.

Lamperti, F., Dosi, G., Napoletano, M., Roventini, A., & Sapio, A. (2018). Faraway, so close: Coupled climate and economic dynamics in an agent-based integrated assessment model. *Ecological Economics, 150*, 315–339.

Lamperti, F., Dosi, G., Napoletano, M., Roventini, A., & Sapio, A. (2020). Climate change and green transitions in an agent-based integrated assessment model. *Technological Forecasting and Social Change, 153*, 119806.

Lamperti, F., Roventini, A., & Sani, A. (2018). Agent-based model calibration using machine learning surrogates. *Journal of Economic Dynamics and Control, 90*, 366–389.

Landes, D. S. (1969). *The unbound Prometheus: Technological change and industrial development in Western Europe from 1750 to the present*. Cambridge University Press.

Lane, D. A. (1993). Artificial worlds and economics, part i and ii. *Journal of Evolutionary Economics, 3*, 89–107 and 177–197.

Lavoie, M. (2009). *Introduction to post-Keynesian economics*. Palgrave Macmillan.

Lavoie, M., & Stockhammer, E. (Eds.). (2013). *Wage-led growth*. Palgrave Macmillan.

Leary, M. (2009). Bank loan supply, lender choice, and corporate capital structure. *The Journal of Finance, 64*, 1143–1185.

LeBaron, B., & Tesfatsion, L. (2008). Modeling macroeconomies as open-ended dynamic systems of interacting agents. *American Economic Review, 98*, 246–250.

Leijonhufvud, A. (1968). *On Keynesian economics and the economics of Keynes: A study in monetary theory*. Oxford University Press.

Leijonhufvud, A. (2000). *Macroeconomic instability and coordination: Selected essays*. Edward Elgar.

Lengnick, M. (2013). Agent-based macroeconomics: A baseline model. *Journal of Economic Behavior & Organization, 86*, 102–120.

Levine, R. (1997). Financial development and economic growth: Views and agenda. *Journal of Economic Literature*, 688–726.

Lindé, Smets, F., & Wouters, R. (2016). Challenges for central banks' macro models. In J. B. Taylor & H. Uhlig (Eds.), *Handbook of macroeconomics*. North Holland.

Lown, C., & Morgan, D. (2006). The credit cycle and the business cycle: New findings using the loan officer opinion survey. *Journal of Money, Credit, and Banking, 38*, 1575–1597.

Lucas, R. E. (2003) Macroeconomic priorities. *American Economic Review, 93*, 1–14.

Lucas, R. E., & Sargent, T. J. (1978). After Keynesian macroeconomics. In *After the Phillips curve: Persistence of high inflation and high unemployment.* Federal Reserve Bank of Boston.

Machlup, F. (1952). *The economics of sellers' competition: Model analysis of sellers' conduct.* Johns Hopkins University Press.

Malerba, F., & Orsenigo, L. (1995). Schumpeterian patterns of innovation. *Cambridge Journal of Economics, 19*, 47–65.

Mandel, A., Jaeger, C., Fuerst, S., Lass, W., Lincke, D., Meissner, F., Pablo-Marti, F., and Wolf, S. (2010). Agent-based dynamics in disaggregated growth models (CES Working Paper No. 2010.77). Université Paris 1 Panthéon Sorbonne.

Mankiw, G. N., & Romer, D. (Eds.). (1991). *New Keynesian economics.* MIT Press.

Mantel, R. (1974). On the characterization of aggregate excess demand. *Journal of Economic Theory, 7*, 348–353.

Massaro, D. (2013). Heterogeneous expectations in monetary DSGE models. *Journal of Economic Dynamics & Control, 37*, 680–692.

Mendoza, E., & Terrones, M. (2012). An anatomy of credit booms and their demise (Working Paper No. 18379). National Bureau of Economic Research.

Metcalfe, J. S. (1994a). Competition, Fisher's principle and increasing returns to selection. *Journal of Evolutionary Economics, 4*, 327–346.

Metcalfe, J. S. (1994b). Evolutionary economics and technology policy. *The Economic Journal, 104*, 932–944.

Minsky, H. (1986). *Stabilizing an unstable economy.* Yale University Press.

Mishkin, F. S. (2007). Will monetary policy become more of a science (Working Paper No. 13566). National Bureau of Economic Research.

Montagna, M., & Kok, C. (2016). Multi-layered interbank model for assessing systemic risk (Working Paper Series No. 2121). European Central Bank.

Moss, S. (2008). Alternative approaches to the empirical validation of agent-based models. *Journal of Artificial Societies and Social Simulation, 11*, 5.

Muth, J. F. (1961). Rational expectations and the theory of price movements. *Econometrica, 29*, 315–335.

Napoletano, M. (2018). A short walk on the wild side: Agent-based models and their implications for macroeconomic analysis. *Revue de l'OFCE, 3*, 257–281.

Napoletano, M., Roventini, A., & Sapio, S. (2006). Are business cycles all alike? A bandpass filter analysis of the Italian and US cycles *Rivista Italiana degli Economisti, 1*, 87–118.

Nelson, R. R., & Winter, S. G. (1982). *An evolutionary theory of economic change*. Belknap Press.

Orphanides, A., & Williams, J. C. (2008). Robust monetary policy with imperfect knowledge. *Journal of Monetary Economics, 54*, 1406–1435.

Pasinetti, L. L. (1974). *Growth and income distribution: Essays in economic theory*. Cambridge University Press.

Pasinetti, L. L. (1983). *Structural change and economic growth: A theoretical essay on the dynamics of the wealth of nations* (Vol. 7). Cambridge University Press.

Pavitt, K. (1984). Sectoral patterns of technical change: Towards a taxonomy and a theory. *Research Policy, 13*, 343–373.

Pesaran, H. M., & Chudik, A. (2014). Aggregation in large dynamic panels. *Journal of Econometrics, 178*, 273–285.

Phelps, E. S., & Winter, S. G. (1970). Optimal price policy under atomistic competition. In E. S. Phelps (Ed.), *Microeconomic foundations of employment and inflation theory*. Norton.

Piketty, T., & Zucman, G. (2014). Capital is back: Wealth-income ratios in rich countries, 1700–2010. *Quarterly Journal of Economics, 129*, 1155–1210.

Poledna, S., Miess, M. G., Hommes, C., & Rabitsch, K. (2023). Economic forecasting with an agent-based model. *European Economic Review, 151*, 104306.

Ponomarenko, A., & Sinyakov, A. (2018, March). Impact of banking supervision enhancement on banking system structure: Conclusions from agent-based modeling. *Russian Journal of Money and Finance, 77*(1), 26–50.

Poudyal, N., & Spanos, A. (2013). Confronting theory with data: Model validation and DSGE modeling (Working Paper). Department of Economics, Virginia Tech.

Prigogine, I. (1980). *From being to becoming: Time and complexity in the physical sciences*. W. H. Freeman & Co.

Raberto, M., Ozel, B., Ponta, L., Teglio, A., & Cincotti, S. (2019). From financial instability to green finance: The role of banking and credit market regulation in the Eurace model. *Journal of Evolutionary Economics, 29*, 429–465.

Ramsey, F. P. (1928). A mathematical theory of saving. *The Economic Journal, 38*, 543–559.

Ratner, D., & Sim, J. W. (2022). *Who killed the Phillips curve? A murder mystery* (Finance and Economics Discussion Series No. 2022-028). Board of Governors of the Federal Reserve System (U.S.).

Reinhart, C., & Rogoff, K. (2009). The aftermath of financial crises. *American Economic Review, 99*, 466–472.

Romer, P. (1990). Endogenous technical change. *Journal of Political Economy, 98*, 71–102.

Romer, P. (2016). The trouble with macroeconomics. *The American Economist*.

Rosser, B. J. (2011). *Complex evolutionary dynamics in urban-regional and ecologic-economic systems: From catastrophe to chaos and beyond*. Springer.

Rotemberg, J. (2008). Behavioral aspects of price setting, and their policy implications (Working Paper No. 13754). National Bureau of Economic Research.

Saari, D., & Simon, C. P. (1978). Effective price mechanisms. *Econometrica, 46*, 1097–1125.

Salle, I., & Seppecher, P. (2018). Stabilizing an unstable complex economy on the limitations of simple rules. *Journal of Economic Dynamics and Control, 91*, 289–317.

Salle, I., & Yıldızoğlu, M. (2014). Efficient sampling and meta-modeling for computational economic models. *Computational Economics, 44*, 507–536.

Sargent, T. J. (2005). An interview with Thomas J. Sargent (CESifo Working Paper No. 1434). Interviewed by G. W. Evans and S. Honkapohja. Available at www.cesifo.org/en/publications/cesifo-working-papers

Schmitt-Grohé, S., & Uribe, M. (2000). Price level determinacy and monetary policy under a balanced-budget requirement. *Journal of Monetary Economics, 45*, 211–246.

Seppecher, P. (2012). Flexibility of wages and macroeconomic instability in an agent-based computational model with endogenous money. *Macroeconomic Dynamics, 16*, 284–297.

Shimer, R. (2005). The cyclical behavior of equilibrium unemployment and vacancies. *American Economic Review, 95*, 25–49.

Silverberg, G., Dosi, G., & Orsenigo, L. (1988). Innovation, diversity and diffusion: A self-organization model. *The Economic Journal, 98*, 1032–1054.

Simon, H. A. (1955). A behavioral model of rational choice. *The Quarterly Journal of Economics, 69*, 99–118.

Simon, H. A. (1959). Theories of decision-making in economics and behavioral science. *American Economic Review, 49*, 253–283.

Simon, H. A. (1977). *An empirically based microeconomics*. Cambridge University Press.

Sims, C. A. (2010). Rational inattention and monetary economics. In B. M. Friedman & M. Woodford (Eds.), (Vol. 3, pp. 155–181). Elsevier.

Smets, F., & Wouters, R. (2003). An estimated dynamic stochastic general equilibrium model of the euro area. *Journal of the European Economic Association, 1*, 1123–1175.

Smets, F., & Wouters, R. (2007). Shocks and frictions in US business cycles: A Bayesian DSGE approach. *American Economic Review, 97*, 586–606.

Solow, R. M. (1956). A contribution to the theory of economic growth. *Quarterly Journal of Economics, 70*, 65–94.

Solow, R. M. (1990). *The labor market as a social institution*. Blackwell.

Solow, R. M. (2005). Reflections on growth theory. *Handbook of Economic Growth, 1*, 3–10.

Solow, R. M. (2008). The state of macroeconomics. *Journal of Economic Perspectives, 22*, 243–246.

Solow, R. M. (2018). A theory is a sometime thing. *Review of Keynesian Economics, 6*, 421–424.

Sonnenschein, H. (1972). Market excess demand functions. *Econometrica, 40*, 549–556.

Steffen, W., Rockström, J., Richardson, Lenton, T. M., Folke, C., Liverman, D., Summerhayes, C. P., Barnosky, A. D., Cornell, S. E., Crucifix, M., Donges, J. F., Fetzer, I., Lade, S. J., Scheffer, M., Winkelmann, R., and Schellnhuber, H. J. (2018). Trajectories of the Earth system in the Anthropocene. *Proceedings of the National Academy of Sciences, 115*, 8252–8259.

Stiglitz, J. E. (1994). Endogenous growth and cycles. In Y. Shionoya & M. Perlman (Eds.), *Innovation in technology, industries, and institutions: Studies in Schumpeterian perspectives*. The University of Michigan Press.

Stiglitz, J. E. (2011). Rethinking macroeconomics: What failed, and how to repair it. *Journal of the European Economic Association, 9*, 591–645.

Stiglitz, J. E. (2012). *The price of inequality: How today's divided society endangers our future*. W. W. Norton and Company.

Stiglitz, J. E. (2014). Reconstructing macroeconomic theory to manage economic policy (Working Paper No. 20517). National Bureau of Economic Research.

Stiglitz, J. E. (2015). Towards a general theory of deep downturns (Working Paper No. 21444). NBER.

Stiglitz, J. E. (2017). Structural transformation, deep downturns, and government policy (NBER Working Papers No. 23794). National Bureau of Economic Research

Stiglitz, J. E. & Weiss, A. (1992). Credit rationing in markets with imperfect information. *American Economic Review, 71*, 393–410.

Stock, J., & Watson, M. (1999). Business cycle fluctuations in U.S. macroeconomic time series. In J. Taylor & M. Woodford (Eds.), *Handbook of macroeconomics* (pp. 3–64). Elsevier, Amsterdam, The Netherlands.

Storm, S., & Naastepad, C. W. M. (2012a). *Macroeconomics beyond the Nairu.* Cambridge MA, Harvard University Press.

Storm, S., & Naastepad, C. W. M. (2012b). *Wage-led or profit-led supply: Wages, productivity and investment* (Conditions of Work and Employment Series No. 36). ILO.

Taylor, J. (2007). The explanatory power of monetary policy rules (Working Paper No. 13685). National Bureau of Economic Research.

Teglio, A., Mazzocchetti, A., Ponta, L., Raberto, M., & Cincotti, S. (2019). Budgetary rigour with stimulus in lean times: Policy advices from an agent-based model. *Journal of Economic Behavior & Organization, 157*, 59–83.

Tesfatsion, L. (2006). Ace: A constructive approach to economic theory. In L. Tesfatsion & K. Judd (Eds.), *Handbook of computational economics ii: Agent-based computational economics.* North Holland.

Turner, A. (2010). The crisis, conventional economic wisdom, and public policy. *Industrial and Corporate Change, 19*, 1317–1329.

Turrell, A. (2016). Agent-based models: Understanding the economy from the bottom up. *Bank of England Quarterly Bulletin, Q4.*

Valente, M. (2008). Laboratory for simulation development - LSD (LEM Working Papers Series No. 2008/12). Scuola Superiore Sant'Anna.

Walde, K., & Woitek, U. (2004). R&D Expenditure in G7 countries and the implications for endogenous fluctuations and growth. *Economic Letters, 82*, 91–97.

Wieners, C., Lamperti, F., Dosi, G., & Roventini, A. (2024). Macroeconomic policies for rapid decarbonization, steady economic transition and employment creation. Available at ResearchSquare.

Windrum, P., Fagiolo, G., & Moneta, A. (2007). Empirical validation of agent-based models: Alternatives and prospects. *Journal of Artificial Societies and Social Simulation, 10*, 8.

Winker, P., Gilli, M., & Jeleskovic, V. (2007). An objective function for simulation based inference on exchange rate data. *Journal of Economic Interaction and Coordination, 2*, 125–145.

Wolf, S., Furst, S., Mandel, A., Lass, W., Lincke, D., Pablo-Marti, F., & Jaeger, C. (2013). A multi-agent model of several economic regions. *Environmental Modelling & Software*, *44*, 25–43.

Woodford, M. (1990). Learning to believe in sunspots. *Econometrica*, *58*, 277–307.

Woodford, M. (2003). *Interest and prices: Foundations of a theory of monetary policy*. Princeton, NJ, Princeton University Press.

Woodford, M. (2013). Macroeconomic analysis without the rational expectations hypothesis. *Annual Review of Economics*, *5*, 303–346.

Woodford, M. (2018). Monetary policy analysis when planning horizons are finite. In *NBER Macroeconomics Annual 2018, volume 33*. University of Chicago Press.

Wright, I. (2005). The duration of recessions follows an exponential not a power law. *Physica A: Statistical Mechanics and Its Applications*, *345*, 608–610.

Yellen, J. (2014). *Monetary policy report to the Congress*. Board of Governors of the Federal Reserve System.

Zarnowitz, V. (1985). Recent works on business cycles in historical perspectives: A review of theories and evidence. *Journal of Economic Literature*, *23*, 523–580.

Zarnowitz, V. (1997). Business cycles observed and assessed: Why and how they matter (Working Paper No. 6230). NBER.

Acknowledgements

We wholeheartedly thank all the colleagues and friends that have contributed to develop the family of the Keynes meeting Schumpeter models, and in particular Giorgio Fagiolo, Francesco Lamperti, Mauro Napoletano, Marcelo Pereira, Tania Treibich, and Maria Enrica Virgillito, who have co-authored most of the works we heavily draw upon in this Element. The success of the K+S modelling enterprise has been our collective result. We thank two anonymous referees for their insightful comments. Last but not least, we thank Isabel Almudi for having encouraged us to write this Element, providing us precious support and help.

Cambridge Elements

Evolutionary Economics

John Foster
University of Queensland

John Foster is Emeritus Professor of Economics and former Head of the School of Economics at the University of Queensland, Brisbane. He is Fellow of the Academy of Social Science in Australia, Life member of Clare Hall College, Cambridge and Past President of the International J.A. Schumpeter Society.

Jason Potts
RMIT University

Jason Potts is Professor of Economics at RMIT University, Melbourne. He is also an Adjunct Fellow at the Institute of Public Affairs. His research interests include technological change, economics of innovation, and economics of cities. He was the winner of the 2000 International Joseph A. Schumpeter Prize and has published over 60 articles and six books.

Isabel Almudi
University of Zaragoza

Isabel Almudi is Professor of Economics at the University of Zaragoza, Spain, where she also belongs to the Instituto de Biocomputación y Física de Sistemas Complejos. She has been Visiting Fellow at the European University Institute, Columbia University and RMIT University. Her research fields are evolutionary economics, innovation studies, environmental economics and dynamic systems.

Francisco Fatas-Villafranca
University of Zaragoza

Francisco Fatas-Villafranca is Professor of Economics at the University of Zaragoza, Spain. He has been Visiting Scholar at Columbia University and Visiting Researcher at the University of Manchester. His research focuses on economic theory and quantitative methods in the social sciences, with special interest in evolutionary economics.

David A. Harper
New York University

David A. Harper is Clinical Professor of Economics and Co-Director of the Program on the Foundations of the Market Economy at New York University. His research interests span institutional economics, Austrian economics and evolutionary economics. He has written two books and has published extensively in academic journals. He was formerly Chief Analyst and Manager at the New Zealand Treasury.

About the Series

Cambridge Elements of Evolutionary Economics provides authoritative and up-to-date reviews of core topics and recent developments in the field. It includes state-of-the-art contributions on all areas in the field. The series is broadly concerned with questions of dynamics and change, with a particular focus on processes of entrepreneurship and innovation, industrial and institutional dynamics, and on patterns of economic growth and development.

Cambridge Elements

Evolutionary Economics

Elements in the Series

A Reconsideration of the Theory of Non-Linear Scale Effects: The Sources of Varying Returns to, and Economics of, Scale
Richard G. Lipsey

Evolutionary Economics: Its Nature and Future
Geoffrey M. Hodgson

Coevolution in Economic Systems
Isabel Almudi and Francisco Fatas-Villafranca

Industrial Policy: The Coevolution of Public and Private Sources of Finance for Important Emerging and Evolving Technologies
Kenneth I. Carlaw and Richard G. Lipsey

Explaining Technology
Roger Koppl, Roberto Cazzolla Gatti, Abigail Devereaux, Brian D. Fath, James Herriot, Wim Hordijk, Stuart Kauffman, Robert E. Ulanowicz and Sergi Valverde

Evolutionary Games and the Replicator Dynamics
Saul Mendoza-Palacios and Onésimo Hernández-Lerma

The Dynamic Metacapabilities Framework: Introducing Quantum Management and the Informational View of the Firm
Harold Paredes-Frigolett and Andreas Pyka

Entrepreneurship and Evolutionary Economics
Per L. Bylund

Agent-Based Macroeconomics: The Schumpeter Meeting Keynes Models
Giovanni Dosi and Andrea Roventini

A full series listing is available at: www.cambridge.org/EEVE

For EU product safety concerns, contact us at Calle de José Abascal, 56-1°, 28003 Madrid, Spain or eugpsr@cambridge.org.

www.ingramcontent.com/pod-product-compliance
Ingram Content Group UK Ltd.
Pitfield, Milton Keynes, MK11 3LW, UK
UKHW040249200625
459886UK00007B/168